Lord, I Hurt So Much!

Frank Cordova

Copyright © 2011 by Frank Cordova

Lord, I Hurt So Much!
by Frank Cordova

Printed in the United States of America

ISBN 9781619044173

All rights reserved solely by the author. The author guarantees all contents are original and do not infringe upon the legal rights of any other person or work. No part of this book may be reproduced in any form without the permission of the author. The views expressed in this book are not necessarily those of the publisher.

Unless otherwise indicated, Bible quotations are taken from The King James Version. Copyright © 1983 by Holman Bible Publishers; and The HOLY BIBLE, NEW INTERNATIONAL VERSION®. Copyright © 1973, 1978, 1984 by International Bible Society.

www.xulonpress.com

Contents

Dedications vii
Introduction ix

Unit I   Lord, I Feel So Low!
Chapter 1   God Loves You Very Much 13
Chapter 2   God's Whispers 20

Unit II   Lord, Help Me To Change!
Chapter 3   Is Evil A Relative Concept? 29
Chapter 4   Jesus, You Endured The Cross,
             Show Me How To Carry Mine 36
Chapter 5   Show Me How To Forgive 41
Chapter 6   Disappointed With God 49
Chapter 7   Trials 55

Unit III   A Changed Life!
Chapter 8   The Turtle Cannot Fly 63
Chapter 9   More Than Conquerors 73
Chapter 10   Time To Let Go 81
Chapter 11   The God Of Love And Peace
             Will Be With You 87

Credits 91

Thanks to...

God the Father for loving us so much that He sent his only Son.

Our Lord and Savior Jesus Christ for washing away all our sins through His precious sacrifice.

Our Comforter and Councilor, the Holy Spirit for His guidance and inspiration.

My loving family:

The love of my life and wife for 25 years, Gloria; for your love and patience and always being by my side.

My precious son Frank Carlos; for your inspirations and also the giving of your talents and dedication to our beloved country in the United States Air Force and in the medical field to help others.

My precious miracle daughter Jasmine Marie; for your laughter and gifts in helping others and bringing joy and hope to everyone around.

Our cherished pastors that we have known for twenty years, Pastor Billy and Bettye Nickell, for setting great examples that we can follow.

Judge Pat Pirtle, Pat and Debby Murphy, for your special friendship and "talking me into" doing prison ministry where I have seen so many of God's miracles.

Barb Thompson for your countless hours of going over my scripts and correcting my grammar.

Shaun and DeeAnn Maxwell for helping me so much with the book cover.

In memory of my beloved parents Charlie and Olivia Cordova

I love all of you
God Bless You!

Introduction

You probably picked up this book because of the picture in the front cover: a broken-hearted man seeking God in prayer, wanting all the pain to stop or the woman seeking God, wanting to find comfort in her afflictions and hardships! You probably picked this book up because of the title: "Lord, I hurt so much!" You probably hurt so much and you don't know what to do. You're at the end of your rope, you've hit rock bottom and you're running out of ideas.

First of all, let me tell you God loves you very much! It may seem at this time that God is so distant, but believe me He isn't. I want to tell you that He wants the best for you even though at this time, it may not seem that way.

Romans 12:15 (KJV) says - *Rejoice with them that do rejoice, and weep with them that weep.*

I want to help you. I want to say that I am with you and I want to mourn with you. I tell you the truth, I have been hurt so deeply by people that I thought were my friends, by family members and if that don't beat all, I have even been hurt by Christian people! Yes, by Christian people. But before someone tries to justify their negative outlook on Christians, let me say that Christians are not perfect, just forgiven. A Christian that follows the Lord Jesus Christ and repents from their sins is fully cleansed by the precious blood of the Lord Jesus Christ! Period.

The purpose of this book is to help you get over the hurt that you are feeling. If someone hurt you by saying mean and untruthful things about you, I want to help you. If someone has stolen your dreams or has stolen your vision and they receive a promotion because they present it as his or her own and it just breaks your heart, I want to help you. If you feel like you have just been overlooked constantly and you feel like there is no future for you, I want to help you. You may have been hurt physically or emotionally, I want to help you. You may have had a death in the family or someone that was close to you passed away; or maybe you yourself have even had suicidal thoughts, I want to help you with your grief. For any reason that you feel hurt, I want to help you.

Let's pray together ok?
Dearest God in heaven, I love you so much and even though right now I feel like you are so far away, the author of this book has told me that you love me very much. Even though I may not feel it at this moment, I do want to say that I trust you. You have a plan for me and it's a good plan. Right now I hurt so much because of certain things that have happened or are now taking place, and they hurt so much! Lord, can you touch my heart and see how I feel at this moment, please? This is how I feel, but I don't want to carry this in me. This does not come from you. Please remove it. I want to feel your love and your peace; your peace that surpasses all understanding. Please wipe away my tears and bring me joy. I want to be like the psalmist that said, "You have turned my mourning into dancing". I love you Lord, please help me, in Jesus' name. Amen.

Unit I

Lord, I Feel So Low!

One thing have I desired of the LORD, that will I seek after;
that I may dwell in the house of the LORD all the days of my life,
to behold the beauty of the LORD, and to enquire in his temple.
For in the time of trouble he shall hide me in his pavilion:
in the secret of his tabernacle shall he hide me;
he shall set me up upon a rock.
And now shall mine head be lifted up above mine enemies
round about me: therefore will I offer in his tabernacle sacrifices
of joy;
I will sing, yea, I will sing praises unto the LORD.

Psalm 27:4-6 (KJV)

Unit I - Chapter 1

God Loves You Very Much

*And we have known and believed
the love that God hath to us.
God is love;
and he that dwelleth in love dwelleth in God,
and God in him.
I John 4:16 (KJV)*

There is a poem that came out some time ago that I want to share with you. You may have already heard it or read it, but here it is again. If you will be seeing it for the first time, I believe you will learn from it. May your heart be touched and your hurts begin to mend. The poem goes like this:

Footprints in the Sand

*One night I dreamed I was walking along the beach with the Lord.
Many scenes from my life flashed across the sky.
In each scene I noticed footprints in the sand.
Sometimes there were two sets of footprints,
other times there were one set of footprints.*

> This bothered me because I noticed
> that during the low periods of my life,
> when I was suffering from
> anguish, sorrow or defeat,
> I could see only one set of footprints.
>
> So I said to the Lord,
> "You promised me Lord,
> that if I followed you,
> you would walk with me always.
> But I have noticed that during
> the most trying periods of my life
> there have only been one
> set of footprints in the sand.
> Why, when I needed you most,
> you have not been there for me?"
>
> The Lord replied,
> "The times when you have
> seen only one set of footprints in the sand,
> is when I carried you." [1]

As the poem explains, at the times when we feel like we are so alone, when we feel like nobody understands or cares; the Lord is actually with us. Think about it, the Bible says in **1 John 4:16** that God is love. God not only loves, he *is* love! Let's look at how the Bible describes love in **1 Corinthians 13, verses 4 - 8a** (NIV):

> Love is patient, love is kind. It does not envy, it does not boast, it is not proud. It is not rude, it is not self-seeking, it is not easily angered, it keeps no record of wrongs. Love does not delight in evil but rejoices with the truth. It always protects, always trusts, always hopes, always perseveres. Love never fails.

If we were to replace the word "love" with "God" in the above verses, it would describe God. It would describe God's love - God's love for you and me. I would especially like to emphasize the last sentence, "it always protects, always trusts, always hopes, always perseveres. Love never fails". God is love, he always protects us. Be assured that like the poem says "The times when you have seen only one set of footprints in the sand, is when I carried you", he is carrying you! You might say, "Well I don't feel him. Why do I hurt so much? Why did he allow someone to hurt me so much if he is protecting me"? These are legitimate questions, but let me ask these questions:

Can there be a victory without a battle? Can you know what you are made of without going through a test? Can you see the best in you without having to go through a conflict?

There are times when we do have to go through things so we can be stronger and better. Stronger and better in our faith, stronger and better to help others, stronger and better to serve God!

How can an athlete know how good he or she is without a race? How can a weight lifter know how much he or she can lift without putting weights on the barbell? How can you know if the person you are going to marry is going to love you for the rest of your life without any type of test?

Before my wife and I got married, we dated for about four and a half years. When we broke up after the first few months, it was devastating! I was a new Christian and I asked the question, "How can a Christian hurt another person"? Gloria was already a Christian and had been for some time. She was a leader in the church and I couldn't understand how she could hurt me so much. But after we broke up and started talking again, things came out in the open and then I understood. She explained that she wasn't ready for a commitment because we were too young; she felt like we were being rushed into getting married by our peers. She was right. When we got back together, our love for each other was stronger and we didn't let the people around us talk us into getting married.

Not too long after that, Gloria told me that she and her sister were moving to California so she could go to cosmetology school. She explained that her relatives had learned that there were more opportunities for her in Los Angeles to obtain a free scholarship to go to a particular school. We lived in Texas so we didn't know about the grants and scholarships in California. Nonetheless, she moved and again my heart was greatly broken. We loved each other deeply, but how could a relationship hold together being so far away from each other? It held together for several months until she told me that she was going to stay in Los Angeles another year so her sister could go to the same cosmetology school. Gloria explained that her sister was working when she was going to school and now it was her turn to work while her sister went to school.

I remember going to Los Angeles the first time to visit her. The California atmosphere set with her so well. Gloria was beautiful, but somehow California just made her blossom! Oh how beautiful she was when I saw her! My best friend Abel, who later on became my best man at our wedding, went with me to L.A. He also commented how beautiful she was.

When Gloria announced that she was going to stay in L.A. another year, things went from bad to worse. Then, when I thought things couldn't get any worse, we broke up again. I hurt so much! I felt a great emptiness! I thought that Gloria was the one. I thoroughly believed that we had a future. She was the strongest Christian I knew; the most consecrated female Christian in the congregation and alongside her beauty, she was such a hard worker. Oh, and to top it off, she was an excellent cook! She was perfect. I was heartbroken. Then, sometime later, a huge bomb dropped in my already broken heart - her sister told me that a great looking, popular guy at her school wanted to take her out. I think that they dated once or twice but Gloria found out that he wasn't for her. During this time, yes, I prayed, "Lord, help me". The pain of a broken heart is so painful! The emptiness of longing for someone that is so loved and imagining life without them is so difficult. Seeing their face everywhere, their smile, hearing their laughter, but they're not there, it's very painful.

I remember that throughout that time though I began praying more, reading the Bible and I discovered a Christian program on TV that was helping me out so much. This program came on around 11:00 pm; the preacher's name was John Osteen. Oh how he could preach! So powerful! He was so encouraging and I could tell how much he loved God and he would always emphasize how God healed his wife Dodi from cancer. My faith started to grow at this time. God sent Brother John Osteen into my life for encouragement, for building up my faith and for bringing me closer to my Lord and Savior Jesus Christ, even though it was only through the television. I remember that my broken heart changed so much. No longer did I feel the pain and the emptiness but I actually felt like great rivers of joy were flowing from my heart!

Joy is a feeling that comes from deep within. It says that no matter what is around us, no matter what the circumstance, it will prevail, it will flow. It is like a shield against negative things that attack you; it just makes them bounce off. Joy flows out and keeps a brightness in your face and doesn't let you focus on the doom and gloom, but it focuses on the creator of life - God Almighty!

Well, Gloria and I started talking on the phone again. Through time, I decided to go visit her in Los Angeles again. I flew there and one of her uncle's asked me to stay at his house so I wouldn't have to spend money on a hotel. He was a great Christian man that God also put in my path. Gloria and I had some great conversations. Then, the time was perfect; we were at a park in L.A. that was close to the house where she and her sister were living. The California sun was shining, the birds were singing, there was love in the air, I asked her to marry me and she said, "Yes"! At that time, I changed her name from Gloria to Glori (glory - because God had blessed me with her and because she was so beautiful, but I changed the "y" to an "i" and came up with Glori). And like the saying goes, "the rest is history."

God knows the timing. He knows what is best for us. He knows who, what, when, where and how. He loves us so much! Glori was to be my wife and we would have a beautiful family together, but certain things had to happen first. God will not hold back anything that is good for us. He loves us. He knows *what* is best for us and *when* things are best for us. There are times that we go through trials, but it just makes us stronger.

Would I have become a stronger Christian without the heartbreaks? I really don't think so. Would I have felt the rivers of joy flowing from my heart without breaking up with Glori? No. Would I have discovered the encouraging preaching of Pastor John Osteen without feeling pain? Probably not. How can someone find encouragement if a person is not looking for it? And if we haven't learned to seek encouragement, then how can one give it when a friend or a relative needs encouragement? How can we teach it to our children or even our parents when they need it?

If we let ourselves be molded like clay in the potter's hands, it's amazing what we can become.

If we let God shape us in the way he wants to shape us and we become the man or woman that he want us to be, then we can bear that same fruit in leading others. It's like the Olympics where one person carries the torch then lights the torch of the next runner and in turn that person passes the flame and lights the next runner's torch until they get to the final destination. Finally, the last person lights the giant cauldron with the fruit of the same flame that is carried by many.

God loves you so much and no matter what you are going through, he is carrying you and he will shape you into the best person that you can be if you let him. I encourage you, keep your chin up. Pray to him, God will listen. Also, seek a great Christian model and encourager and the rivers of joy will begin to flow from your heart. And I said rivers, not little streams, rivers; they will flow from deep within. It is a great feeling, believe me, I say it from experience. God loves you so much!

Prayer: *Lord, thank you for carrying me, I need it so much. My energy is so drained with all that I am going through; I really do need to be held up. Hold me with your strong arms. Lord, I have learned that you will give me rivers of joy. Lord, this is what I seek. If I am to go through these trials, then make me strong so that I can learn what it is that I am supposed to learn through this. Shape me into the person you want me to be, and Lord, when the* situation arises and I see others go through the same things, let me be an encourager in their lives and help me to tell them about your greatness! And Lord, thank you for loving me so much, in Jesus' name, amen.

Unit I - Chapter 2

God's Whispers

*After the earthquake came a fire,
but the Lord was not in the fire.
And after the fire
came a gentle whisper.*
I Kings 19:12 (NIV)

The verses for this chapter come from I Kings. The story begins on chapter 18 of I Kings when the prophet Elijah wanted to meet with Ahab the king of Israel at that time. Elijah challenged Ahab to summon all the four hundred and fifty prophets of Baal and the four hundred prophets of Asherah, the pagan gods that king Ahab and his wife Jezebel had turned to; and not only them but a great portion of the nation of Israel. All of them were assembled on Mount Carmel and Elijah asked a great question, *"How long will you waver between two opinions? If the Lord is God, follow him; but if Baal is God, follow him."* – **I Kings 18:21** (NIV). Elijah put out a challenge and gave the instructions to get two bulls to sacrifice, one for the pagan prophets and one for Elijah. Each was to prepare their bull for the sacrifice and put them on the wood but none was to light the wood. After this, in **verse 24**, Elijah said, *"Then you call on the name of your god, and I will call on the name of the Lord. The god who answers by fire—he*

is God." All the people agreed, then the prophets of Baal began calling on Baal from the morning until noontime and nothing happened. At that time Elijah began to make fun of them: **verses 27-29** – *At noon Elijah began to taunt them and the Baal prophets shouted even louder and cut themselves until the evening.* Then it was Elijah's turn. He made an altar to the Lord, put the sacrifice on it, and dug a trench around it. He gave instructions to pour water on the sacrifice three times and the water was so much that it flowed down and filled the trench. I love the verses that follow: **I Kings 18:36-39** (NIV)

At the time of sacrifice, the prophet Elijah stepped forward and prayed: "O Lord, God of Abraham, Isaac and Israel, let it be known today that you are God in Israel and that I am your servant and have done all these things at your command. Answer me, O Lord, answer me, so these people will know that you, O Lord, are God, and that you are turning their hearts back again." Then the fire of the Lord fell and burned up the sacrifice, the wood, the stones and the soil, and also licked up the water in the trench. When all the people saw this, they fell prostrate and cried, "The Lord—he is God! The Lord—he is God!"

What a great victory! But sadly, it was short lived for as soon as King Ahab told his wife Jezebel, she sent a message to the prophet Elijah that he would be killed for doing what he did, since after the great victory Elijah had all the prophets of Baal killed. When Elijah heard this, he ran for his life into the desert and prayed for God to take his life; he didn't want to live anymore! Elijah fell asleep but an angel woke him up and told him to eat. As Elijah looked around, he saw that the angel brought him some bread and water. He ate the bread and drank the water but he still went back to sleep. A second time, the angel of the Lord woke up Elijah and told him to get up and eat. Elijah ate, drank, got up and traveled for forty days and forty nights. He finally arrived at Mount Horeb and he went into a cave. There, the Lord asked him, *"What are you doing here, Elijah?"* – **I Kings 19:9b**. Elijah answered by trying to explain that the people of Israel had rejected God and had broken down his altars. He further added that he was the only prophet left and to top it off, they were trying to kill him. At that moment, God spoke to Elijah, **verse 11** – *The Lord said, "Go out and stand on the mountain in the presence of the Lord, for the Lord is about to pass by."* The story continues:

> *Then a great and powerful wind tore the mountains apart and shattered the rocks before the Lord, but the Lord was not in the wind. After the wind there was an earthquake, but the Lord was not in the earthquake. After the earthquake came a fire, but the Lord was not in the fire. And after the fire came a gentle whisper. When Elijah heard it, he pulled his cloak over his face and went out and stood at the mouth of the cave. Then a voice said to him "What are you doing here, Elijah?"*

Elijah again answered the same thing as before, how the people of Israel had rejected God, broken down his altars and how he was the only prophet left, plus, they were trying to kill him. Even though Elijah was depressed and felt worthless, the Lord did something extraordinary – the Lord gave Elijah three missions: he was to go out and anoint three people – anoint two people to be kings and one to be a prophet; God still wanted to use him! God still had plans for him! God didn't put him down and told him to get over himself! Then, almighty God, the God of love, encouraged Elijah and told him that there were seven thousand people in Israel that had not bowed down to Baal nor had kissed him.

This was the God that Elijah served, the same God that we serve, worship and praise now! This is how much God loved Elijah and how much he loves us too! Notice that when Elijah had thoughts of dying and when he couldn't take it anymore and fell asleep, God Almighty sent him food and water. God provided for him and took care of him. God understands what we go through and he loves us so much he wants to meet our needs and help us. He is there for us and with us, no matter how low we feel. Even when Elijah had a great victory where many people at Mount

Carmel recognized that the Living God was the true God when the Lord answered his prayer, Elijah still went through a very difficult time. Many people that were there and even now as people read this story would say to Elijah, "How can you fall into such deep depression when the Lord just gave you a great victory?" Most people would probably give him such a hard time. But not God, not our loving God, our God strengthened him! In the above verses, when Elijah was in a cave and God told him to come outside where the presence of the Lord was about to pass by, the Bible says that a great and powerful wind split the mountains and broke the rocks into pieces, but the Lord wasn't in the wind. Then after that, there was an earthquake but the Lord wasn't in the earthquake either, and then came a fire, but the Lord wasn't in the fire either. To me, in these verses God says:

> "Is there anything too great for me to handle? Is there any mountain I can't move or for that matter, split it in two? Is there any storm that I can't calm? Is there anything on earth that I can't control? Is there any fire that I can't put out? IS THERE ANY PROBLEM THAT I CAN'T HANDLE?"

The answer always comes back, "No" a big "NO!" There is nothing that Almighty God can't handle! Dearest brother or sister, whatever problem you have, turn it over to God, he will handle it. In fact, we are commanded in **1 Peter 5:7** (NIV) – *Cast all your anxiety on him because he cares for you.* Yes, because he cares for you! God is powerful enough to do anything, but notice that God also came in a gentle whisper. It was a gentle caressing whisper that encompassed Elijah and encouraged him to take on the next tasks.

Let me tell you another time when God's gentle voice spoke - a special time when God's whisper touched my heart. One day, one of my friends that got me into prison ministry named Debby and I were talking about the Lord and the conversation focused on forgiveness. I said something like, "I can forgive when others do harm to me, but there are times when it's so hard to forgive myself. But then I pray to God, ask for help and he touches my heart and before I know it, he whispers a song into my heart." And Debby said, "Wow that really touched my heart. That should be a song." The Lord was giving me songs during that time and I would always picture the Lord whispering them into my heart. That evening when I went home and picked up my guitar, the Lord whispered a new song in my heart, I called it "God's Whispers" and it goes like this:

God's Whispers

*There's times when I don't
know what I would do,
if Your voice was not there,
to lead me and guide me through!*

*There's times when I don't,
know where I would start,
if your voice was not there,
speaking into my heart!*

1st chorus:
*'Cause hearing your voice,
hearing your melody,
feeling your love,
a new song then comes to me!*

*You come in the night,
you whisper in my heart,
all the words I should write,
to tell all how much you care!*

*There's times when I don't
know what I would do,
if your voice was not there
to lead me and guide me through!*

2nd chorus:
'Cause through all that I've done,
through all of my failures,
your forgiveness is there,
and I'm cleansed through your Holy blood!

You're faithful and true,
you lead me and guide me,
you love has no end,
you're eternal and Holy!

Bridge:
Thank you dear God,
for all the songs that you have given me.
And I thank you dear God,
for all the sins that you have forgiven me!

And I thank you dear God,
for all your blessings and provisions.
But most of all my God,
I thank you for my salvation!

God's gentle whisper filled me with his precious love. As the song explains, there are times when we don't know what to do, we know we have failed and the problems just seem to get bigger and bigger, but John tells us in **1 John 1:9** (KJV) – *If we confess our sins, he is faithful and just to forgive us our sins, and to cleanse us from all unrighteousness.* Don't be hard on yourself if you have messed up. The word of God tells us in **Romans 3:23** *(KJV) – For all have sinned, and come short of the glory of God.* Let's get up, dust ourselves off and go on!

Let me close this chapter with this verse from **Romans 5:8** (NIV) – *But God demonstrates his own love for us in this: While we were still sinners, Christ died for us.*

When did Jesus die for us? While we were yet sinners. When did Jesus love us? While we were yet sinners!

Prayer: *Oh Lord, thank you that even when I fail and I feel worthless, you are there for me, you lift me up and strengthen me. You demonstrate to me that there is nothing too great that you can't handle and you show me this in many ways, yet you speak to me in a gentle whisper and show me that you can still use me and that you still have a plan for me; a good plan! With your strength I will get back up, dust myself off and follow you. I love you very much, in Jesus' name, amen.*

Unit II

Lord, Help Me To Change!

God, grant me the serenity to accept the things I cannot change, courage to change the things I can, and wisdom to know the difference.
Living one day at a time; enjoying one moment at a time; accepting hardship as a pathway to peace; taking, as Jesus did, this sinful world as it is, not as I would have it; trusting that You will make all things right if I surrender to Your will; so that I may be reasonably happy in this life and supremely happy with You forever in the next. Amen[1]

Reinhold Neibuhr

Unit II - Chapter 3

Is Evil A Relative Concept?

*Fret not thyself because of evildoers,
neither be thou envious
against the workers of iniquity.
Psalm 37:1 (KJV)*

Here is a question for us: Is evil a relative concept? In other words, what I believe to be evil is it evil to someone else? For example, most people would agree that stealing is evil, after all it is stated as one of the Ten Commandments in the Bible, **Exodus 20:15** (KJV) - *Thou shalt not steal*. So, for argument's sake let's say that you believe that stealing is evil, I believe that stealing is evil and of course, God almighty says it's evil. So, the bottom line, stealing is evil.

What about cheating on a test? Is that evil? If the instructions on the test specifically say NOT to use any help from any type of material and NOT to talk to anybody during the exam, but someone decides to do it, to me that is evil. But let's say that one of the persons taking the exam uses outside material or speaks to his neighbor that is also taking the exam or this person says something like, "This is the way I learn", is this then considered cheating? If he or she continues his or her argument saying, "I need this certification" or "I need this license", does the end justify the means? Is this considered cheating? Is this considered evil?

I also believe that people that live in luxury with new houses and new cars and love to receive free things yet don't give to the poor or the homeless is evil. They live in abundance but are usually looking for a way for someone else to pay for their meals or trips because they're "important." Then, when these rich individuals are approached to help the homeless, they will use an excuse like, "Oh, they might use the money for the wrong reasons, so I don't give!" If I believe that this is evil, but other people do not, then is it evil? In other words, is evil a relative concept?

Many people have seen movies, read books or have experienced it in real life where someone comes up with an idea or an invention and a "friend" runs away with it, becomes rich and is admired by the world. Others take the credit for what someone else did, and when upper management sees the work and is very pleased by it, the one who took the credit is promoted. When it is explained that this wasn't their original work, that it was copied from someone else, it rarely does any good. Is this evil or is it survival of the fittest?

My friend, if someone takes your invention or idea and steals it and calls it his or her own, this is evil. Asaph, the psalmist struggled with this very concept in **Psalm 73:1-10** (NIV).

Surely God is good to Israel, to those who are pure in heart. But as for me, my feet had almost slipped; I had nearly lost my foothold. For I envied the arrogant when I saw the prosperity of the wicked. They have no struggles; their bodies are healthy and strong. They are free from the burdens common to man; they are not plagued by human ills. Therefore pride is their necklace; they clothe themselves with violence. From their callous hearts comes iniquity; the evil conceits of their minds know no limits. They scoff, and speak with malice; in their arrogance they threaten oppression. Their mouths lay claim to heaven and their tongues take possession of the earth. Therefore their people turn to them and drink up waters in abundance.

This psalm describes the wicked so adequately; they have such a callous heart to where they don't feel remorse anymore, and consequently *"the evil conceits of their minds know no limits"*.

When I was eighteen, I went to live with my oldest sister in New Mexico for a while. My sister Sadie and her family lived out in the country. Even though they had the many conveniences of modern electricity and gas, they preferred to have a wood-burning stove to heat the house; therefore we had to chop wood in the fall so the family could have enough wood for the winter. The first time I joined the men to chop wood, the axe made blisters on my hands because of the constant sliding motion of the axe handle against the skin of my palms. I wasn't used to this type of work so my hands were sensitive. At first I felt pain and I didn't want to do that kind of work anymore. Then, as the days passed and I kept chopping wood, my hands became calloused; the skin on my hands became hard and tough. The sensitivity was gone.

The same thing happens to a person that becomes wicked. At first, when he or she hurts someone, the sensitivity is still there and he or she will feel bad. Apologies for doing wrong still exist at this level. Then as time progresses and the evil continues, he or she becomes calloused in his or her heart. Their heart becomes hard and the apologies are replaced with excuses. Then as the psalmists says in verse 7, *"From their callous hearts comes iniquity; the evil conceits of their minds know no limits."*

At this point, the psalmist is dismayed and wonders why he has kept his heart pure if the wicked prosper greatly and get away with evil. But Asaph continues in verse **16-28** (NIV).

When I tried to understand all this, it was oppressive to me till I entered the sanctuary of God; then I understood their final destiny. Surely you place them on slippery ground; you cast them down to ruin. How suddenly are they destroyed, completely swept away by terrors! As a dream when one awakes, so when you arise, O Lord, you will despise them as fantasies. When my heart was grieved and my spirit embittered, I was senseless and ignorant; I was a brute beast before you. Yet I am always with you; you hold me by my right hand. You guide me with your counsel, and afterward you will take me into glory. Whom have I in heaven but you? And earth has nothing I desire besides you. My flesh and my heart may fail, but God is the strength of my heart and my portion forever. Those who are far from you will perish; you destroy all who are unfaithful to you. But as for me, it is good to be near God. I have made the Sovereign Lord my refuge; I will tell of all your deeds.

At first, it seems like the wicked get away with their evil deeds, then Asaph describes their final destiny - God will cast them down to ruin. Asaph continues in comforting the reader by saying God holds us by our right hand and guides us. He then exalts God Almighty and promises to tell all of His mighty deeds.

In **Matthew 23:12** (NIV), it says: *For whoever exalts himself will be humbled, and whoever humbles himself will be exalted.*

James 4:10 (KJV) - *Humble yourselves in the sight of the Lord, and he shall lift you up.*

There are things in this life that we cannot change. There will always be evil people doing what they do best – evil. These include bullies, unjust managers, crooked politicians, people from corporations that lie about their earnings, etc. They will hurt people and many times enjoy doing it. Plus, they often believe that they are getting away with it.

If you have been hurt by some of these people, be encouraged, God sees it and He will take care of it. God loves you! **Psalms 68:19** (NIV) – *Praise be to the Lord, to God our Savior, who daily bears our burdens.*

The Lord sees all this, the Lord sees the injustice, the Lord sees your hurt. But one thing that you have to understand brother or sister is that God will take care of the situation. Let's read a few verses that the Holy Spirit inspired to write in the Bible.

Romans 12:19-21 (NIV)- *Do not take revenge, my dear friends, but leave room for God's wrath, for it is written: "It is mine to avenge; I will repay, "says the Lord. On the contrary: "If your enemy is hungry, feed him; if he is thirsty, give him something to drink. In doing this, you will heap burning coals on his head." Do not be overcome by evil, but overcome evil with good.*

Proverbs 20:22 (NIV) - *Do not say, "I will repay evil"; Wait for the LORD, and He will save you.*

2 Timothy 4:14 (KJV)- *Alexander the coppersmith did me much evil; the Lord reward him according to his works.*

Hebrews 10:30-31 (KJV) - *For we know him that hath said, Vengeance belongeth unto me, I will recompense, saith the Lord. And again, The Lord shall judge his people. It is a fearful thing to fall into the hands of the living God.*

On the following chart, compare what the world says to what the word of God says. Even though we cannot change what some people do or believe, we can see what God's word says. God will take care of the situations. Let us submit our lives to God Almighty and His holy ways.

Philippians 4:8-9 (NIV) - *Finally, brothers and sisters, whatever is true, whatever is noble, whatever is right, whatever is pure, whatever is lovely, whatever is admirable—if anything is excellent or praiseworthy—think about such things. Whatever you have learned or received or heard from me, or seen in me—put it into practice. And the God of peace will be with you.*

Topic	What the world says	What the Bible says
Dishonest gain	Everybody does it. You have to do it if you want to get ahead in life. They did it to you; you should do it to them.	**Exodus 18:21** (NIV) - But select capable men from all the people — men who fear God, trustworthy men who hate dishonest gain...
Gaining popularity by making fun of others	It's fun! Ah, I was just joking! Oh, can't you just take a joke, you're so touchy! Oh, you're just too delicate!	**Matthew 7:12** (NIV) - So in everything, do to others what you would have them do to you... **Ephesians 5:4** (NIV) - Nor should there be obscenity, foolish talk or coarse joking, which are out of place, but rather thanksgiving
Cheating on tests	Cheating is just a part of life. This is the only way I can pass these tests. Everybody does it.	**Deuteronomy 25:16** (NIV) - For the Lord your God detests anyone who does these things, anyone who deals dishonestly.

Prayer: *Beloved Lord God Almighty, I love you. You are so wonderful. You are my deliverer. You defend me from all evil, you are my fortress. There are things and people in my life that I cannot change, and I have been hurt by their actions. I try to shake them off, but I just see these actions as evil and so unjust and I can't do anything about them. So I ask you to change **me**. Change me to where these things don't affect me anymore Lord. Help me* *to put these things in your hands and leave them there and be fully trusting in you that you will take care of things. You are our beloved Father in heaven; in you I put my trust. Help me to overcome evil with good; with your goodness, with your precious love, in the name of your beloved son Jesus Christ, amen.*

Unit II - Chapter 4

Jesus, You Endured The Cross Show Me How To Carry Mine

*Let us fix our eyes on Jesus, the author and perfecter of our faith,
who for the joy set before him endured the cross,
scorning its shame, and sat down at the right
hand of the throne of God.
Consider him who endured such opposition from sinful men,
so that you will not grow weary and lose heart.
Hebrews 12:2-3 (NIV)*

We learn in this chapter from the Lord Jesus how he endured the cross and gain strength from him. When a close friend of mine hurt me so deeply that I fell into deep depression, part of my prayer was to ask the Lord for strength. I would ask him for the same strength that he had focused on when he endured all the torture, all the mocking, carrying the cross and finally the crucifixion with nails through his hands and feet. The night that the Lord Jesus was arrested, he was betrayed by one of his disciples; a follower, someone close to him. A large crowd was sent from the chief priests with swords and clubs to take Jesus and arrest him. As these men stepped forward to seize the Lord, one of the disciples drew his sword and cut off the ear of the servant of the high priest. He was trying to defend Jesus and protect him, but surprisingly Jesus told him to put away his sword and asked, *"Do you think I cannot call on my Father, and he will at once put at my disposal more than twelve legions of angels"?* - **Matthew 26:53** (NIV). The Lord Jesus was very well protected, but he chose to fulfill scripture, he chose to proceed with the plan of salvation. He would suffer, die and redeem mankind, fulfilling all the scriptures about him.

When I fell into depression, it was so difficult to not focus on the pain. It affected my thoughts, my work, and even my spiritual life. I would start to pray, but the hurt in me was so deep that I couldn't even complete the sentences in my prayers. I would try to begin but only a few words would come out of my mouth, then I would just fall asleep with my face down on the carpet. As the days progressed, I remember asking the Lord, "Lord, give me the same strength that you had when you endured all the torture, when you endured the mocking from your very creation, when you endured all the suffering on the cross". The Lord honored those prayers and he did pick me up from that depression. I'll explain more of what I went through and how I felt in Chapter 8.

As you are going through some kind of hurt; some kind of pain that possibly brings you to depression like I felt, let this be your prayer also. Ask Jesus to give you the strength and the focus that he had as he endured all that he suffered – "Jesus, you endured the cross, show me how to carry mine."

From our chapter verses, the author of the Book of Hebrews shows us that our Lord Jesus Christ was focused on the joy set before him. He could see beyond the pain that he was going through physically as he was beaten so many times and nails penetrated the hands that healed so many - those hands that held children, multiplied food, and performed so many miracles. He focused on the joy set before him, beyond the pain that he was going through emotionally as his very creation was mocking him. He focused on the joy set before him and beyond the physical pain as a crown of thorns was placed on his head. His body endured so much pain from being whipped many times and ultimately, the pain of being crucified. Yet Jesus looked beyond the torment and the shame of the cross, and endured it all. No wonder the author of the book of Hebrews tells us to fix our eyes on the Lord Jesus Christ. Indeed, he is the author and perfecter of our faith. He is our model. And looking at his very example, our faith is increased! The last sentence of our reading, *"Consider him who endured such opposition from sinful men, so that you will not grow weary and lose heart"*, is powerfully encouraging. I cannot tell you as a step by step process or offer a formula as to how this is conceived, but I can tell you that Jesus shows us and helps us in a unique way that is individualized to each person. Only he can do that. As I have stated, "This was my prayer when I was hurt by a very close friend and brother in Christ". Jesus pulled me out of that depression and strengthened me. I believe it is an individual case with each person and we should let the Lord Jesus mold us to what he wants us to be molded into.

Let me explain. There is the story in the Book of Daniel chapter three when king Nebuchadnezzar, the king of Babylon made a huge image of gold and commanded everyone to bow down to it when the music started playing and anyone who did not fall down and worship the image would be thrown into a fiery furnace. Well, when the music played and the people fell down and worshipped the golden image, some people came to the king to tell him that there were some Jews that did not bow down and worship the king's golden image. That made king Nebuchadnezzar very angry and he demanded to know who they were and the response was Shadrach, Meshach and Abednego. King Nebuchadnezzar had them brought in and asked them if it was true that they didn't bow down to his golden image and gave them one more chance to fall down and worship his golden image when all the musicians played and warned them again that if they didn't, they would be thrown into a fiery furnace and Nebuchadnezzar added, "Then what god will be able to rescue you from my hand?" (The last sentence in **Daniel 3:15**). Afterwards, **Daniel 3:16-18** (NIV) states:

> *Shadrach, Meshach and Abednego replied to the king, "O Nebuchadnezzar, we do not need to defend ourselves before you in this matter. If we are thrown into the blazing furnace,*

the God we serve is able to save us from it, and he will rescue us from your hand, O king. But even if he does not, we want you to know, O king, that we will not serve your gods or worship the image of gold you have set up."

Shadrach, Meshach and Abednego trusted in their God, the true God; the living God Almighty. They trusted that God would save them from the blazing furnace *but... ... ...and this is what I love... ... ...but* even if he didn't save them from the blazing furnace, they would not serve the gods of Nebuchadnezzar or worship his golden image. They understood that if they had to go into the blazing furnace, if they had to go through what they had to go through, God in the end would still be with them.

Sometimes we go through and into the fiery furnace to see what we are made of and also to see the mighty hand of God at work and this makes us stronger! In the case of Shadrach, Meshach and Abednego they didn't get burned when they were thrown into the fiery furnace, even though the king ordered the furnace to be heated seven times hotter than usual. The three were tied and thrown in but when king Nebuchadnezzar looked into the furnace, he saw **four** people and declared that the fourth looked like "the Son of God" (KJV). When Nebuchadnezzar called them out, the Bible continues:

> *They saw that the fire had not harmed their bodies, nor was a hair of their heads singed; their robes were not scorched, and there was no smell of fire on them.* – **Daniel 3:27** (NIV)

They went into the fiery furnace but God was with them. God is with us, God is with you! Take courage, God is with you!

I believe that Jesus' joy that was set before him was that he would die for all of us and all of us that receive him as savior would be over-comers just like him. He taught us to keep our focus on the promises of God as he kept his focus and now sits at the right hand of the throne of God. Even through all his sufferings, being laughed at, being emotionally and physically hurt, he still kept his focus on what would be accomplished in the end.

"Consider him who endured such opposition from sinful men, so that you will not grow weary and lose heart." Don't lose heart. I am a witness to being able to overcome with the help of the Lord. I love what **Hebrews 11:32-34** (NIV) says:

> And what more shall I say? I do not have time to tell about Gideon, Barak, Samson, Jephthah, David, Samuel and the prophets, who through faith conquered kingdoms, administered justice, and gained what was promised; who shut the mouths of lions, quenched the fury of the flames, and escaped the edge of the sword; whose weakness was turned to strength; and who became powerful in battle and routed foreign armies.

Again, it tells us about gaining the promises of God and tells about the great things that they did by the power of the Lord and ultimately, their weakness was turned to strength!

God Almighty will strengthen you my brother! God Almighty will strengthen you my sister! When I prayed for Jesus to help me and to give me strength, it didn't happen overnight, it took some time. For me it probably took a several weeks, but through each step as God made me stronger, my prayer life became stronger and God showed me several things throughout that journey. Enjoy the journey with God as well, take joy in this too! Let's pray.

Prayer: *Precious beloved Lord Jesus, you endured the cross; your very creation mocked you and hit you. Your closest friends ran away when you were in trouble and one even denied that he knew you. You were betrayed and the people that should have realized who you were, they were the very ones that wanted to kill you. But Lord Jesus, you kept your focus, you died for my sins to redeem me, you showed me how to overcome, you showed me that all the promises in the Bible are true and that they are for me also. Thank you for giving me strength for when I have to go through things and Lord, I will keep my mind and my heart open to what I have to learn as I go through trials. I will carry my cross and I will keep my focus in your promises, with your strength. I love you, in your Holy name, Amen.*

Unit II - Chapter 5

Show Me How To Forgive

*And forgive us our debts,
as we forgive our debtors.
Matthew 6:12 (KJV)*

My wife Glori, my daughter Jasmine and I have been involved with prison ministry for about eleven years. There were three people that got me involved in this ministry: a district court judge, his court reporter and the court reporter's husband. I worked on computers so they would call me to work on theirs when they would have problems. After a short time, I noticed that that judge Pirtle was a Christian and so was his court reporter Debby. Debby had several crosses, Bible verses and Christian pictures in her office. One day, as I was fixing her computer, we started talking about church and the Lord Jesus Christ. We had a very edifying talk that day and later on she introduced me to her husband Pat who happened to be an assistant district attorney. They told me about the prison ministry that they were involved with and told me that the judge had just lead the last group that ministered at a local maximum security prison. All three of them "ganged up on me" to join them in this ministry and I finally gave in. They told me that they would minister to the inmates by showing them the love of the Lord Jesus Christ. The ministry team would take short sermons that they called "talks" and a lot of great food and lots and lots of cookies. The inmates were called "brothers in white" since the mandatory clothes at the prison were all white. After going to some meetings for training and getting to know the rest of the team, we went into the prison. It turned out to be one of the greatest ministries that I have ever served in; this is where I have seen the greatest miracles in my life – in prison!

I have seen gang leaders that hated each other so much but when God got a hold of them they were crying and hugging each other and were asking each other for forgiveness. Yes, you read this correctly; they hugged each other and asked each other for forgiveness. Only God Almighty can do this! Time and time again, I have seen big tough inmates that come in with so much hate and a hard heart. Later, they are weeping so hard because the Lord just washed away their sins and all the hate and anger are gone as God replaces them with love and peace! I have witnessed white-supremists hug their black brothers (and vice-versa) when God touches their heart and removes all the hate.

Forgiveness is an amazing thing when God is behind it and honestly, I believe that true forgiveness can only be through the Lord Jesus Christ. It takes his precious Holy power to let go of the hate and the thoughts of revenge that unforgiveness brings.

Another thing that is always so amazing to experience is when the inmates discover that one of the persons on the team is actually a district court judge. When they see him they'll say something like, "Hey wait a minute that's the guy that put me in here, that's the guy that sentenced me and put me in here!" Of course, they didn't put it in such a mild language as this. As the days progress and the inmates see the love of Jesus in us and in the judge, they realize that we really are there for them in the love of the Lord. It's amazing to see when the inmates begin to trust the judge and some even hug him. Judge Pirtle is ok with it and even tells them, "This is a good time to take the law into your own hands!" So they hug him and since he's a judge they 'take the law into their own hands!'

We have such a great time in the Lord! At first, the inmates blame the judge for putting them there, but later the inmates realize that it was because of what they did that they wound up in prison. The way they feel towards the judge is evident through their hugs—forgiveness! Wait a minute, didn't we say it wasn't the judge's fault that the inmates were in this maximum-security prison but it was because of what the inmates did? Yes, but in their minds, the judge was to blame; the judge was guilty and bitterness and thoughts of revenge set in, but when God delivered them from those thoughts and those walls came down, forgiveness came in along with love and peace.

It's so amazing how the "brothers in white" testify of how they feel God's love and forgiveness, how God has washed away all their sin. They also testify about how they have even forgiven themselves. Some "brothers in white" struggle with forgiving themselves for what they did, but our Almighty and Powerful God can wash this away also. Forgiveness, it's a great feeling! Forgiveness!

When Jesus taught his disciples to pray, the Lord Jesus taught them this prayer that is found in **Matthew 6:9-13** (KJV):

Our Father which art in heaven,
Hallowed by thy name.
Thy kingdom come.
Thy will be done in earth, as it is in heaven.
Give us this day our daily bread.
And forgive us our debts,
as we forgive our debtors.
And lead us not into temptation,
but deliver us from evil:
For thine is the kingdom,
and the power, and the glory,
for ever. Amen.

The Lord also continued in **verses 14 and 15** (KJV) saying:

> *For if ye forgive men their trespasses, your heavenly Father will also forgive you: But if ye forgive not men their trespasses, neither will your Father forgive your trespasses.*

When we look closely at the prayer, it says, "forgive us our debts, *as* we forgive our debtors", we put the emphasis on "as". This then becomes a condition, as we do something, the result unfolds. In this case, as we forgive, we are forgiven. The Lord Jesus continues to elaborate on this in verses 14 and 15 with the word "if" – if we forgive those that wronged us, our heavenly Father will also forgive us, but if we don't, then we won't be forgiven for the things that we do!

I believe that that's why we feel such a great weight lifted from us when we forgive. The heaviness of all the thoughts of revenge and hate goes away and the Lord replaces it with his precious peace. Some people go through so many years not talking to someone that has wronged them and the sad thing is that it happens even with relatives. There are sons and daughters that don't talk to their parents and vice-versa or other relatives because of a disagreement, resentment or anger. I have noticed though, that when these type of people let God in and forgiveness takes over, they usually hug each other and cry. I believe crying "washes" the soul. It's a cleansing that washes away all the ugly weight that we had in our heart and all the chains are broken; all the walls are torn down.

Besides forgiveness, there is another word that comes to my mind as the Lord Jesus Christ gave the Sermon on the Mount in Matthew chapter 5. The word that comes to my mind is "reconciliation"; to settle our quarrels. Let us read what Jesus said in **Matthew 5:21-24** (KJV):

> *Ye have heard that is was said by them of old time, Thou shalt not kill; and whosoever shall kill shall be in danger of the judgment; But I say unto you, That whosoever is angry with his brother without a cause shall be in danger of the*

judgment: and whosoever shall say to his brother, Raca, shall be in danger of the council: but whosoever shall say, Thou fool, shall be in danger of hell fire. Therefore if thou bring thy gift to the altar, and there rememberest that thy brother hath ought against thee; Leave there thy gift before the altar, and go thy way; first be reconciled to thy brother, and then come and offer by gift.

Several things stand out in these verses but let me emphasis on just two. First of all there is being angry with your brother (or sister) without a cause. It does not profit a thing to be angry just for the sake of being angry. As human beings there will be times when we won't agree on all issues, but we can "agree to disagree", meaning both parties have spoken their point of view and both have their strong convictions and neither is going to budge. This is not out of stubbornness, but out of conviction; a true belief deep down in the heart.

There is a good example in the Bible where out of conviction, a deep rooted belief, two very good friends parted ways. We take up the story in **Acts 15:36-40** (NIV):

Some time later Paul said to Barnabas, "Let us go back and visit the brothers in all the towns where we preached the word of the Lord and see how they are doing." Barnabas wanted to take John, also called Mark, with them, but Paul did not think it wise to take him, because he had deserted them in Pamphylia and had not continued with them in the work. They had such a sharp disagreement that they parted company. Barnabas took Mark and sailed for Cyprus, but Paul chose Silas and left, commended by the brothers to the grace of the Lord.

To me, the apostle Paul was a "go-getter, bottom-line, let's get it done, no-nonsense" type of person. When Mark deserted Paul on another journey where they were spreading the gospel, it didn't settle too well with Paul. Paul was focused on what needed to be done and he didn't like the idea of someone quitting before the job was completed. On the other hand, I believe Barnabas was an encourager (his name actually means son of encouragement), he had compassion, a person of "let's give him another chance" type of person. It wasn't so much that each didn't have the other personality traits, but I'm speaking more of what was the dominant personality.

On the missionary trip that they were about to take, Barnabas wanted to take Mark but Paul didn't. The Bible says that *"they had such a sharp disagreement that they parted company."* They both had success in their journeys with the companions they chose and the gospel was preached, plus, the people were encouraged - this was the original plan.

The emphasis in this story is that Paul and Barnabas "agreed to disagree". They both had a strong conviction - a true belief deep down in their hearts. From these convictions, they both parted ways but still set out to accomplish what was originally planned. In addition to that, Barnabas also wanted to give Mark a second chance, another opportunity to prove himself, and Mark did.

We received the Gospel of Mark as the Holy Spirit inspired him to write it. Paul recognized the new fruit that Mark had and wrote to Timothy in **2 Timothy 4:11** to bring Mark with him because he was helpful in Paul's ministry. In **Colossians 4:10-11**, Paul names Mark as a fellow worker for the kingdom of God and also speaks well of him in being a comfort to him while Paul is in prison. There was reconciliation here and Paul was a true apostle that practiced also what he preached. In **Ephesians 4:26** (KJV), Paul instructs us *to be angry and sin not*. It's ok to be angry but we don't have to hate the person that angered us and have evil thoughts about them, this is the second emphasis that I would like to make.

I believe that Jesus was pointing this out as he commented in the condition of the heart that one has when he or she is angry. Jesus clearly showed that a person doesn't have to kill physically to be under the same danger of judgment as one that is angry with his brother or sister where it takes up a deep root and evil sets in.

In all this, I am thoroughly convinced that Jesus wants us to always be reconciled with each other, where we don't give the devil something to work with. It doesn't necessarily mean that we will agree on every issue, but we can "call it a draw" where we cannot come to an agreement and remain friendly.

I do believe that there is a time to part ways and have nothing to do with a person, (I touch more on this subject in chapter 8, "The Turtle Cannot Fly.") but even then, sin not. The forgiveness is still there, the soul cleansing is still there - sin not. Remember, we are forgiven as we forgive those who trespass against us. We can do this through Jesus Christ our Lord.

Prayer: *Precious Jesus, our Lord and Savior, you are Holy forever and ever. Jesus, you are our perfect model and you taught us how to forgive. Lord, give me that sensitivity in my heart also; to forgive those who trespass against me. I understand that if I want to be forgiven, I must forgive also. The author of this book tells me that with forgiveness comes love and peace. I want that love and peace that can only come from you. I don't want to harbor unforgiveness. I want that weight to be taken off. I now forgive those that hurt me so much. Forgive me for holding on to so much bitterness. I now ask you to come into my heart, in your precious and powerful name, amen.*

My future wife Glori after graduating from cosmetology school in Los Angeles. She sent me this picture with a stuffed puppy named 'Barkley' that I sent her.

Our handsome son Frank helping to defend our country in the United States Air Force.

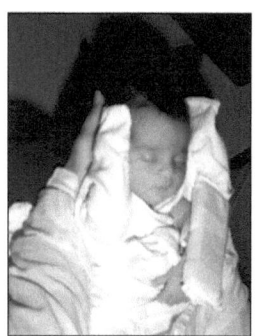

"Perfect Peace." The Lord gave Jasmine perfect peace. Notice there is a brace on her arm to give it support as the doctors gave her so many injections and drew so much blood for tests.

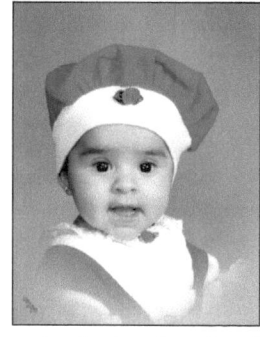

Our miracle daughter Jasmine, with a big beautiful smile[2].

Unit II - Chapter 6

Disappointed With God

*How long shall I take counsel in my soul,
having sorrow in my heart daily?
Psalm 13:2 (KJV)*

Most people, if not all (if we're all willing to admit), have been disappointed with God. Some would say that this is a very harsh statement! But as I have stated, if we are willing to admit, the majority of the human race has been in this situation at some time. If we think back, we could probably find things that we thought should have happened to us but didn't, or things that shouldn't have happened to us but did. If we have listened closely, we probably have heard the phrase, "Why do bad things happen to good people?"

One of the saddest and most difficult things to understand is when someone close to us dies, especially when a child or a baby dies. As innocent as they are, delicate, sweet, never hurt anybody, never did anything 'bad', why are they taken from us so soon?

I never met an older sister that I had; she died before I was born. I remember seeing her in a picture and asking my mother about her. In the black and white photo was my mother holding a beautiful little baby girl and beside them was my aunt comforting my mom as they were preparing for the baby's funeral. The way my mother explained it to me, the baby's father was a very mean individual that made her suffer very much. He physically abused my mom and made her go through many difficult situations and consequently, she developed strong negative emotions that built up inside her like anger, fear, depression, etc. Throughout all this, my mother was breast-feeding the baby and somehow the breast milk became as a poison to the baby and the baby died. A few years ago, I was telling this story and a highly educated woman began to tell me that the same thing happened to her and nobody would believe her. Like my mother, she was convinced that in the midst of all the abuse, her body reacted in such a way that it created a "poison" in the breast milk and it affected the baby and the baby died.

At times like this, we tend to wonder, how did the wickedness of one man and the suffering of one woman result in the life of an innocent child ending? How was it the fault of a baby? Why did God take the baby away?

One day as I was driving home, I heard a woman crying on the radio when she called a Christian radio station asking for prayer and comfort. She and her husband had been so happy that they were going to have a baby but around her second month of pregnancy, she had a miscarriage. She cried so much. I prayed together with the announcer as he led her in prayer. Our hearts truly went out to her as we were listening to her story while she was crying. She stated that she was disappointed with God. Yet through her tears she sincerely expressed love for God.

It's a very difficult time when we lose a loved one. I lost both my parents some time ago and I still miss them. For some time after my mother died of cancer, when good things happened to me, I would start to run out the front door to go to my mother's house to tell her about it. All of a sudden, I would remember that she was gone and the emptiness would set in. My father died when I was a little boy and even now, I still miss him very much. Not too long ago, I saw him in a dream. I remember looking up at him with a big smile and I told him that I loved him. He smiled back at me as he did when I was little. As I hugged him and I put my cheek to his, I could feel the stubble on his face, just as I remember when I was a little boy.

I remember crying for my parents. Yet it was different with each one. When my father died, I was about five or six years old and I reacted as a child; I cried and sought comfort where I could. Yet when my mother died, I was about twenty six years old and I knew Jesus as my personal Savior. The Lord gave me strength throughout all this and I could feel his comforting peace - a gentle peace that surpassed all understanding.

I don't know what comfort my mother sought when her baby died, but I would assume that she sought comfort from her siblings. I believe this because one of my aunts was with her in the picture. Although I don't downplay the comfort of family and friends, I do believe that the comfort of God Almighty is different. His loving arms just seem to "take in" a person and the love is overwhelming.

It seems like a contradiction, first blaming God for bad things, yet seeking His Holy comfort. But if we look closely at our lives, how many times do we get upset at the person that we love? We argue, point fingers and blame them for our mishaps, yet later we apologize and we hold each other in comfort. This happens over and over with husbands and wives, friends, siblings and other family members.

I remember that some time after my father died, my mother re-married. At first, everything seemed like we were going to be one big happy family. Then, when I was between the ages of eight and twelve, my step-father would come home drunk very often. We would all be asleep, then, at two or three in the morning, he would come home, pushing his weight around and making huge demands. When my mother didn't give in to his demands, the hitting would start. I can still picture the beatings and the violence that he brought to our family. I remember once, my step-father grabbed my mom around the throat and as she tried to get loose, she fell back unto the couch. I felt I had to do something so I reached for the closest thing to me. I got a hold of a book and threw it at him. It hit him on the head and the impact made him let go of my mom. But then, he turned to me with evil in his eyes and charged at me with great vengeance. He jerked my arm and lifted me up then got a hold of my leg with his other hand and threw me against the floor and I rolled against the TV. When I got up and went to hug my mother to see if she was alright, my step-father seized me by the throat and began to choke me. I remember another time when he was choking my mother and my youngest sister hit him to get him away from my mom and he grabbed her and threw her against the foot of the bed. I can still picture how the back of her little body hit the metal frames. Again I went at him as I tried to defend my family and again his hand was around my throat.

A child shouldn't have to go through these things. A child should not see this kind of violence. A child's life should not be threatened this way. And yet throughout all this, when my mother or one of my sisters would tell my step-father to leave the house, I remember crying with him and begging him not to leave. Was this a contradiction, knowing that the violence came from my step-father and with him being removed, the violence would be gone, yet begging him not to leave? It does seem that way, but love has a way of turning things around. After the forgiveness we would hold each other in comfort. I don't give this illustration as a means for people to tolerate violence because nobody should, especially when there are children involved. But I do give this example to show that this is what happened with us and to point out certain situations that seem to contradict each other.

Some people blame God when things don't go their way. Expressions of anger against God come out as stressful situations escalate. "Why did God allow this to happen?" "God could have stopped this but he didn't!" "If God is a God of love, why is he making me go through this?" Instead of blaming him, I would encourage people to seek him with all their hearts. God *is* a loving God.

Remember the woman that called the radio station for comfort? She called because the pastors in this particular program are very wise and love the Lord. The program is called "To Every Man An Answer"[2]. Every day as I'm driving home from work, I listen to this broadcast where people call in with questions about the Bible or Christianity and the pastors answer the questions with the Bible.

Pastors Mike Kestler and Leo Giovinetti were on that day. They prayed for her and showed her true Christian love. Then they suggested that some of the things that she could do for further comfort were to listen to praise music and praise the Lord whenever she started to feel depressed. They also suggested reading loving scriptures; strengthening scriptures.

I thoroughly agree with the pastors because the word of God gives strength and lifts us up from the most difficult situations. In times of seeking comfort in the word of God, I love to turn to the Book of Psalms. The Psalms were inspired in such a way that they convey emotions that come from deep within the soul. The psalmists have a genuine way of expressing their pain and concerns, then they make known that they find comfort in reading the word of God. At that moment as they find comfort in scripture, they'll also begin to praise the Lord. This is also encouraging because we know that God inhabits the praises of his people (**Psalm 22:3**). With God's presence there, you can fully feel his comfort and his precious hug as his Holy presence encompasses you.

> **Psalm 119:52** (NIV) - *I remember your ancient laws, O LORD, and I find comfort in them.*

> **Psalm 27:13-14** (NIV) - *I am still confident of this: I will see the goodness of the LORD in the land of the living. Wait for the LORD; be strong and take heart and wait for the LORD.*

> **Psalm 30:5b** (NIV) - *weeping may remain for a night, but rejoicing comes in the morning.*

> **Psalm 30:11-12** (NIV) - *You turned my wailing into dancing; you removed my sackcloth and clothed me with joy, that my heart may sing to you and not be silent. O LORD my God, I will give you thanks forever.*

Psalm 34:1-8 (KJV) - *I will bless the LORD at all times: his praise shall continually be in my mouth. My soul shall make her boast in the LORD: the humble shall hear thereof, and be glad. O magnify the LORD with me, and let us exalt his name together. I sought the LORD, and he heard me, and delivered me from all my fears. They looked unto him, and were lightened: and their faces were not ashamed. This poor man cried, and the LORD heard him, and saved him out of all his troubles. The angel of the LORD encampeth round about them that fear him, and delivereth them. O taste and see that the LORD is good: blessed is the man that trusteth in him.*

Psalm 34:18 (NIV) - *The LORD is close to the brokenhearted and saves those who are crushed in spirit.*

Psalm 142:3 (NIV) - *When my spirit grows faint within me, it is you who watch over my way.*

Prayer: *Beloved Lord God Almighty, first of all, forgive me for the times that I have blamed you for the bad things that have happened in my life. I now realize that I can take comfort in you. Instead of turning my back on you, I will turn to you. You are the everlasting God that loves me and cares for me. I will be strong in you and you will turn my wailing into dancing. I trust in you to heal my broken heart. You are my strength, my fortress, my shield and my protector. I love you very much, in Jesus' name, amen.*

Unit II - Chapter 7

Trials

*Consider it pure joy, my brothers,
whenever you face trials of many kinds,
because you know that the testing of your faith
develops perseverance.
Perseverance must finish its work so that
you may be mature and complete,
not lacking anything.
James 1:2-4 (NIV)*

What beautiful verses! James tells us to consider it pure joy whenever we face trials of many kinds. This would of course include trials where someone hurts us, whether we are going through sadness, depression, the loss of someone, the loss of a job, wrong decisions - trials of many kinds.

There are things in life that are very hard to explain why they happen, but in this imperfect world of sin, there are and will be problems, but Jesus our Lord said, *"I have told you these things, so that in me you may have peace. In this world you will have trouble. But take heart! I have overcome the world."* **John 16:33** (NIV)

Jesus will give us peace. Sometimes we have to go through the trials and as James tells us, it will develop perseverance. But here is the promise from the Lord Jesus Christ, that through that trial, He will give us peace! In the times where the pain is unbearable, Jesus promised to give us peace. Jesus may take away the trouble instantly and honestly, those are very great times - from *our* perspective because the pain is gone quickly. But there are other times when we must go through the fire! It is said that silversmiths would heat up the silver in the fire and hammer out the imperfections and impurities of the silver. They would constantly do this until they could see their reflection in the silver, that's when they knew it was pure. Using the same illustration, we are put through the fire and the imperfections and impurities are hammered away through trials until the reflection of Jesus shines on us. That is our goal as Christians, to be more like Jesus.

Perseverance must finish its work so that you may be mature and complete, not lacking anything. Those are powerful words, inspired by the Holy Spirit. In life, the same thing happens; we are born immature and defenseless. A newborn baby cannot feed itself nor take care of itself. It cannot provide its own food, clothing or shelter, but as he or she matures and gets educated in life, then he or she can provide for itself and we can say that he or she is mature. We all get educated in life, whether we are educated by our parents, Sunday school teachers, school teachers or just life in general, we all get our education in one way or another and what we learn makes us who we are through the choices we make. When we (all the human race) are very young and can sit up, we learn to pick up small pieces of food with our little fingers and put them in our mouths, but as we get older, we learn by watching adults or by instructions from adults on how to use a spoon and a fork to eat our food. We mature in our eating habits as we persevere in learning how to use silverware. In the same manner, as we persevere in life and learn from our Lord Jesus Christ, we mature and become complete in Him.

I remember when we got the news that my mother had cancer. My wife Glori, my one year old son Frankie and I were leaving on vacation for a couple of weeks and my mother was showing me something that was on her head. As I touched her head, my heart sank to my feet - she actually had a hole on her skull and when I touched it, my fingers felt the delicate skin on her head push into her skull. I knew it was serious! I asked her if she had gone to the doctor and she said that she had made an appointment. We were going to postpone our vacation trip but she insisted that we should go. When we were on vacation, I called her to ask her what the doctor said and she said that she would tell us in detail when we came back from vacation and told us not to worry and go and have fun. That didn't sound good, but I shook it off. We finally came back home and we went to my mother's house and she told us that she had bad news - she was all full of cancer! Cancer had eaten part of her skull and she also had cancer in her lungs, it was terminal. Needless to say, we prayed and we prayed a lot. Glori would pray with my mother and my mother enjoyed it so much as she said that it was so soothing. My mom enjoyed those times very much and they have been a special memory in my wife. We got the news about the cancer sometime in June or July of that year and by November, she was sleeping most of the day. She kept getting worse and one night, we called the ambulance to take her to the hospital and two days later she passed away.

We prayed for healing for several months. God chose not to heal her in this life, but I'm sure she is healed in heaven. She has no more pain and she suffers no more! She is present with the Lord Jesus Christ (... *to be absent from the body, and to be present with the Lord* **2 Corinthians 5:8b**). This in itself is a great miracle, for about two weeks before she fell into the state of just sleeping, she accepted the Lord Jesus Christ as her personal Savior! This was a prayer that had been prayed many times - for her salvation.

I was saved when I was nineteen years old and by this time when my mother accepted Jesus, I was twenty six. So several years had passed and throughout those years she would always say that she wanted to stay with her traditional beliefs. Persevering in prayer, my beloved mother was saved. She was washed in the blood of the Lord Jesus Christ and her name was written in the Lamb's Book Of Life. What a joy! It was a long time praying, but as I look back at the joy I felt when she accepted the Lord as her Savior it was well worth it. Many years I talked to her about the

Lord. Several others did too, but on that day, God had a special plan to answer that prayer.

Throughout the time when it was discovered that my mother had a terminal illness, I prayed for her healing and I remember emphasizing in my prayers that I couldn't go on without her, I couldn't handle that kind of emptiness. Yet, after she died, several people told me how they saw such a great peace in me. God matured me in this, he was my shelter in time of need, he was my refuge and my strength and up to this day, he still is. This in turn helped out a close friend of mine when his daughter died. He told me later that when his little daughter died, he prayed for the same peace that he saw in me.

I love James' words, *"Consider it pure joy, my brothers, whenever you face trials of many kinds, because you know that the testing of you faith develops perseverance. Perseverance must finish its work so that you may be mature and complete, not lacking anything"*. Our faith is tested and when we pass through that test and come out on the other end, it is a joy. I do rejoice that my mother got saved. Throughout each trial, my faith has become stronger in the Lord. And even when others saw the peace that the Lord gave me, a peace that surpasses all understanding, it also became a witnessing tool that made people say, "I want that in my life also".

Also, when you pass through a trial, at the end, you now have a "testimony!" A testimony that you can share with others that are going through pain and heartaches and you tell them that you went through the same thing but there is a God that helped you out and made you stronger. They'll listen. They'll respond because they want to get through that pain and heartache also and come out stronger.

Read through the Book Of Philippians. The apostle Paul wrote this epistle while he was a prisoner in Rome. Read how many times he wrote the word "joy" or "rejoice". Now how many people can write about joy or rejoicing while being a prisoner? I would say that there are not too many out there. Yet the apostle Paul knew whom he believed in, he knew whom he served, he knew from whom he got his strength - the King of kings and Lord of lords, the Lord Jesus Christ! In this Book of the Bible are Paul's great words of encouragement and strength - *I can do all things through Christ which strengtheneth me*. **Philippians 4:13** (KJV).

Prayer: *Dearest Lord in heaven, I adore you so much. I thank you for the trials that I go through because now I recognize that you will give me the strength to go through them and at the end I will be a better and mature person, my faith will become stronger and I will have a solid witnessing tool - my testimony. And through this testimony I will tell others of your greatness and how you can help them through what they are going through, no matter what the trial is! I love you so much, in Jesus' precious name, amen.*

Unit III

A Changed Life!

*And be not conformed
to this world:
but be ye transformed by the
renewing of your mind,
that ye may prove
what is that good,
and acceptable,
and perfect,
will of God.*

Romans 12:2 (KJV)

Unit III - Chapter 8

The Turtle Cannot Fly

*Blessed is the man who
does not walk in the counsel
of the wicked
or stand in the way of sinners
or sits in the seat of mockers.
Psalm 1:1 (NIV)*

This chapter came to us as Glori and I were talking while we went on a long trip to Mexico. We talked about how sometimes people have gotten upset at others because others don't do things the way one would do them or because others do not explain or say things the way one would say them. We also talked about lack of communication where one person explained a certain situation to a second person but the second person perceived the instructions in a different manner and did the job the wrong way. We began to elaborate on how people are so different and how we perceive things differently sometimes, it's kind of like having the "glass half full of water or half empty" concept. Then my wife said something about how a turtle can't be like a soaring eagle. Then I said, "That would be a great title to one of the chapters, "The Turtle Cannot Fly". So the concept is like this:

The eagle has a bird's eye view of everything around it and below it for many miles. A turtle has a limited view of its surroundings plus poor eyesight and it moves rather slowly to gather information of its environment. So the eagle doesn't think as the turtle does nor does the turtle think like the eagle because each has a different view or perception of how things are.

People come in all shapes and sizes, in all types of personalities and have a different viewpoint of things. Take for example driving from point A to point B. Some people would take the freeway to get there faster; others would take the back roads to avoid the heavy traffic. Neither is wrong per say, but the one that took the freeway would probably reason that it's the fastest and best way to get to the destination but the other would probably argue, "What's the hurry, there's plenty of time!"

So, with this in mind, when we get hurt, could it be a misunderstanding? Could it be that the person who hurt us was trying to communicate something else? Perhaps, there are true sincere people that make honest mistakes. When they come to us with a broken heart and explain what they actually meant and we in turn, with a sincere heart, listen to what they have to say and realize that there was an honest mistake, the relationship is built back up. Sometimes the relationship even becomes stronger, whether it's a friendship, a husband and wife or parent and child. This is even what the Lord wants from us - "a broken and contrite heart". **Psalm 51:16-17** (NIV) – *You do not delight in sacrifice, or I would bring it; you do not take pleasure in burnt offering. The sacrifices of God are a broken spirit; a broken and contrite heart, O God, you will not despise.* A sincere heartfelt "I'm sorry" goes a long way. When the misunderstanding is cleared up, the mistakes that were made should not be repeated so the relationships may grow.

If you were hurt by a possible misunderstanding, I would encourage you to go to that person and ask him or her if they really meant what they said or did. Give him or her chance to explain himself or herself. If it turns out to be a misunderstanding and all is cleared up, then you have mended your relationship and you will be so much happier plus a great weight will be lifted off your shoulders. What you will also learn is to see things in a different perspective and your friend, relative, or spouse will also see your viewpoint. A word of caution here though, do not try to convince each other of how wrong they were, the hurt feelings will come back up and possibly with a greater vengeance! Instead, the bottom line here is to understand each other's viewpoint and learn from them. If things start to get out of hand, a simple "let's just stop there, let's don't hurt each other again" should put things back in order. Don't let things escalate to what first brought the hurt. In **Proverbs 20:3** it says – *It is to a man's honor to avoid strife, but every fool is quick to quarrel.*

Where it gets more difficult is when there is a person that enjoys "pushing people's buttons." This type of person is the "jokester," the one that gets his or her kicks by mocking people and when it escalates to a point of anger from the receiver, he or she then exclaims, "I was just joking" or "Can't you take a joke?" It further complicates things when the people around him or her say something like, "Oh that's just the way 'John' is, you just have to get used to him" or "Oh, you just have to get to know 'Sue', that's just the way she is." Actually the Bible speaks contrary to this.

Titus 3:10 (NIV) – *Warn a divisive person once, and then warn him a second time. After that, have nothing to do with him.*
Notice that it doesn't say to tolerate him or her; it says to have nothing to do with him (or her).

Ephesians 5:4 (NIV) - *Nor should there be obscenity, foolish talk or coarse joking, which are out of place, but rather thanksgiving*

Merriam-Webster dictionary defines the word "divisive" as creating disunity or dissension[1]. A person that likes to push a person's buttons just to get them angry or stirred up is a divisive person, that person creates disunity. I would ask, "How or why would a person enjoy making another person angry and laugh at him or her?" How is it funny to mock another person? Isn't that what they did to our Lord Jesus Christ? They laughed at him, mocked him, placed a crown of thorns on his head and then they hit him and said, "Prophecy to us now, who hit you?"

Again, the wisdom of the Bible tells us in **2 Timothy 2:16** (NIV) – *Avoid godless chatter, because those who indulge in it will become more and more ungodly.* Indeed, only an ungodly person can enjoy teasing and laughing at people all the time! In the fifth chapter of the book of Ephesians, after giving a list of things that are improper for God's holy people, the Bible states in **Ephesians 5:6-7** (NIV) - *Let no one deceive you with empty words, for because of such things God's wrath comes on those who are disobedient. Therefore do not be partners with them.*

I lost a very good friend that I loved as a brother because of this kind of attitude. When things were good, they were very good. When he wasn't trying to push my buttons, the friendship was a very close one. When things would get out of hand, that would be the saying, "I was just joking." After four years of this, our friendship fell apart. Even water can penetrate and break rock when the water drops constantly bang on the solid rock. Constant "put-downs", ridiculing me in front of my peers and my family finally broke my spirit and our friendship took a big hit. With these acts and also breaking our trust in other ways were what thoroughly broke my heart, and consequently, our friendship collapsed.

I couldn't believe some of the things that he did and I fell into a huge depression. For several months I couldn't handle it. Even when I thought some people would help out in the situation, they didn't and that broke my heart even further. I fell into a deep depression and it was so hard to come out of it. Everything around me suffered; my spiritual life, my studies, my work and my family, everything suffered! I remember trying to pray at night and nothing would come out of my mouth. I would start with a few simple words, then nothing. I would lie on the floor faced down with so much hurt and just fall asleep. How could this brother hurt me so much? The words of David from **Psalm 55** (NIV) kept coming to my mind.

Verses 4-8 – *My heart is in anguish within me; the terrors of death assail me. Fear and trembling have beset me; horror has overwhelmed me. I said, "Oh, that I had the wings of a dove! I would fly away and be at rest – I would flee far away and stay in the desert; I would hurry to my place of shelter, far from the tempest and storm.*

Verses 12-14 – *If an enemy were insulting me, I could endure it; if a foe were raising himself against me, I could hide from him. But it is you, a man like myself, my companion, my close friend, with whom I once enjoyed sweet fellowship as we walked with the throng at the house of God.*

Oh how King David described the very words I felt – *"my companion, my close friend, with whom I once enjoyed sweet fellowship as we walked with the throng at the house of God"*. My sorrow went like this for the longest time. I hit rock bottom!

A scene from the *Rocky III*² movie kept playing in my mind. It was the scene where the ex-champion *Apollo Creed* is trying to train *Rocky* for a second boxing match with *Clubber Lang*, played by *Mr. T* so *Rocky* can retain his championship title. *Apollo* and *Rocky* are running in the beach and *Apollo* is trying his hardest to get *Rocky* back in shape, then all of a sudden *Rocky* stops running and his face shows defeat, he doesn't want to continue, he doesn't want to go on, he can't go on, it's over! *Rocky* stops running and turns the opposite way and slowly starts walking with his hands on his waist, just giving up.

That's how I felt, I couldn't go on, my face showed defeat and I would bury it on the floor and nothing would come out of my mouth in my prayers. Then… …oh then, God began to pick me up! Slowly, more and more words were added to my prayers and my prayer life started to change. It became stronger and stronger! Through time, God began to show me new things and I was called to help minister at a little church in Shamrock, Texas where they didn't have a pastor. God Almighty lifted me up from that depression and sorrow and filled me with a stronger prayer life and new sermons. It was like the *Rocky* theme song started playing at this point! God was there to lift me back up, strengthen me and to be the champion in His wonderful plan!

So even though sometimes we get hurt by people that just have a difficult personality, God will somehow use it to build us up into the strong person he wants us to be. We don't understand why some people enjoy hurting others. We don't understand why even our closest brothers and sisters hurt us so profoundly. We just need to know that whatever the devil meant for evil, God will use it to make us a better and stronger person. We learn this from Joseph, the eleventh son of Jacob in the Old Testament.

Jacob was the grandson of Abraham and Jacob had a son that he loved very much named Joseph. Jacob showed a lot of favoritism towards Joseph and this made his other brothers very jealous. When Joseph was a young man, he had dreams about his brothers bowing down to him and he told his brothers about his dreams and these dreams made them even more jealous. Then one day to top it off, Jacob made a beautiful coat for Joseph and sent him to check on his brothers that were tending the flocks. The brothers saw Joseph coming from far away and they devised a plan to kill him, but the older brother talked them out of it and instead they threw him in a pit, then they sold him to some people that were on their way to Egypt. Yes, the brothers actually sold their younger brother!

While in Egypt, Joseph became a servant and was doing well for a while, but his master's wife was attracted to him. When Joseph didn't give in to her desires, she became very angry and claimed that Joseph tried to molest her and as a result, Joseph was thrown into prison for several years. Now Joseph was unjustly put in prison for what he did not do. One day while in prison, two of pharaoh's servants were also cast into prison because they made pharaoh very angry. Not too long after this, the servants were talking about the dreams that they had the previous night and Joseph told them the meaning of their dreams. In the interpretation, Joseph told one of the servants that he would go back to serve pharaoh and continue to be his cupbearer. Joseph also mentioned to the servant to be sure to remember him when he went back to serve pharaoh. The servant was set free, just as Joseph had said, but he forgot about Joseph for two years. Finally, pharaoh had a dream and wanted to know what it meant but nobody could interpret it. At that moment, the servant remembered Joseph and told pharaoh about him and pharaoh sent for him. Joseph interpreted the dream by the power of God and pharaoh was so pleased that he made Joseph second in command in all of Egypt! At that point, Joseph literally went from rags to riches. Joseph got married and sometime later, his wife had two sons: Manasseh and Ephraim. Here is where I want to make an emphasis. In **Genesis 41:50-52** (NIV) it says:

> *Before the years of famine came, two sons were born to Joseph by Asenath daughter of Potiphera, priest of On. Joseph named his firstborn Manasseh and said, "It is because God has made me forget all my trouble and all my father's household." The second son he named Ephraim and said, "It is because God has made me fruitful in the land of my suffering."*

Here is the emphasis: At the time of Joseph's first son, God made him "forget" all his trouble and all his father's household so he named his first son Manasseh. Then, at the time of his second son, Joseph praised God by naming his son Ephraim because God made him fruitful in a land where he suffered so unjustly.

Joseph didn't forget in a state of mind where he couldn't remember how his brothers sold him into slavery and how he was unjustly accused of rape and thrown into prison. It wasn't that he had amnesia and that part of his memory was erased. Rather, he forgot the torment that these situations put him through, in other words, that torment didn't affect him anymore. He moved on with his life. Joseph didn't forget that he went through it, but he didn't dwell on it to where it would bring him down or where he wanted vengeance. This is even evident in naming his second son, for Joseph focused more on the blessings that God had given him in the land of Egypt where he had suffered so much. And again this is true when the famine came and his brothers came to Egypt for food but they didn't recognize their brother Joseph. When Joseph finally told his brothers who he was, his brothers shook with fear. As powerful as Joseph was, he could have motioned for them to be thrown into prison or to be executed. But Joseph made a great statement in **Genesis 45:4-7** (NIV)

> *Then Joseph said to his brothers, "Come close to me." When they had done so, he said, "I am your brother Joseph, the one you sold into Egypt! And now, do not be distressed and do not be angry with yourselves for selling me here, because it was to save lives that God sent me ahead of you. For two years now there has been famine in the land, and for the next five years there will be no plowing and reaping. But God sent me ahead of you to preserve for you a remnant on earth and to save your lives by a great deliverance.*

And again in **Genesis 50:19-20** (KJV):

> *And Joseph said unto them, Fear not: for am I in the place of God? But as for you, ye thought evil against me; but God meant it unto good, to bring to pass, as it is this day, to save much people alive.*

There are people today that would probably say, "If you don't forget, it means that you didn't forgive!" I would say, "Don't fall into that trap brothers and sisters. As humans, we cannot forget, don't fall into that trap. Only God can truly forget and it's not because he has a bad memory, it's because he chooses to." We read this **in Hebrews 8:12** (NIV)

> *For I will forgive their wickedness and will remember their sins no more.*

We learn this also in **Hebrews 10:16-17** (NIV)

"This is the covenant I will make with them after that time, says the Lord. I will put my laws in their hearts, and I will write them on their minds." Then he adds: *"Their sins and lawless acts I will remember no more."*

Joseph didn't dwell on all the hurt, but he took the attitude that what his brothers meant for evil, God used it to do good! That is so encouraging. Even the New Testament takes this approach; we see it in **Romans 8:28** (KJV)

And we know that all things work together for good to them that love God, to them who are the called according to his purpose.

The turtle cannot fly and can't be like a soaring eagle, but God created both of them for his glory. There will be times when our spirit is crushed because of what people say or do, but be encouraged, for what people mean to do for evil, God will use it for good.
In **Proverbs 15:4** (NIV) it says:

The soothing tongue is a tree of life, but a perverse tongue crushes the spirit.

Even though you may have been hurt by what someone has said and your spirit has been crushed, let's you and I focus more on the first part of the Proverb and speak good things. The first part of **Proverbs 18:21** (KJV) says:

Death and life are in the power of the tongue

Let's speak life into people! And we'll also follow what our verse for this chapter is:

> Blessed is the man who does not walk in the counsel of the wicked or stand in the way of sinners
> or sits in the seat of mockers. **Psalm 1:1** (NIV).

Prayer: *My dearest and most precious God, you are amazing! Even when things are bad, you turn them around and make them good. I can now see that there truly is a silver lining in every dark cloud! I choose now to follow your precious ways and not speak or do evil, but rather, I'll speak life and encouragement to people. Thank you for the story of Joseph's life, I have learned so much from him. Help me to forget the pain and torment that someone has caused me. I now choose to embrace your promises instead of embracing the hurt that was caused. I love you so much. Thank you, in Jesus' name, Amen.*

Unit III - Chapter 9

More Than Conquerors

*Nay, in all these things
we are more than conquerors
through him that loved us.
Romans 8:37 (KJV)*

When our son Frankie was a little boy he would tell us how he longed to have a brother or sister. I had gone back to college and during my last year, my wife Glori and I decided that Frankie was right; it was time to have another child. It was March 1995, joy overtook us when we found out that Glori was pregnant with our second child and our baby would be born around my graduation time - December 1995. To add to our joy, we discovered later that we were going to have a little girl!

For spring break of that year, we decided to go to Mexico for vacation. We had a great time during the two weeks that we were there. On the last day, my sister-in-law and her husband took us out to eat and the next day we came back home to Canyon, Texas; a suburb of Amarillo. The following day I went to my classes then went to work and noticed that I began to have very strong pains in my stomach. My co-workers would ask me if I was ok and insisted that I go home and rest. I went ahead and finished my shift and went home, but the pains got worse. Then, about four or five in the morning, Glori took me to the hospital emergency room so they could see what was wrong. I remember feeling such great pain in my stomach as the car hit every little bump and hole on the road. It took the doctors a while to find out what I had but they finally decided to treat it as food poisoning and gave me some strong medication. As the days progressed, Glori also felt nauseated, but we thought it was due to the pregnancy. She started to lose weight, a lot of weight. One day she came home from work feeling very tired and she lay down on the couch shaking, telling me that she was very cold. As I was covering her with a blanket, I looked at her; she had lost so much weight! I covered her with a blanket and she fell asleep. I sat beside her, looking at her and my heart sank! There was much more to this than just the pregnancy. Something wasn't right. I held her and told her to not protest anymore, she needed to go to the doctor.

  The doctor found that Glori was very anemic and checked her into the hospital. She was later transferred by ambulance to a hospital in Amarillo so she could be treated by specialists since she was pregnant. After some time and several tests, the specialists found that Glori's body had been fighting something and it had damaged her liver. Throughout this time, they had been carefully giving her antibiotics at a safe dosage as to not affect the baby. The doctors wanted to combat the sickness that was damaging the liver, but they didn't know what they were up against so they told us that they wanted to do a biopsy, which meant going into the liver with a needle and taking samples. We thought that it was a good idea, but then they told us the bad news - the biopsy could make the liver bleed and cause a chain reaction to other organs to go into some kind of shock and we could lose the baby. So, they basically told us to make a decision - my wife Glori or our baby girl!

  What a decision to make! How do you choose one life over another? From my perspective, how could I make a choice to lose the love of my life or to let go of the life of a little innocent baby girl? It wasn't any easier with Glori and me putting our heads together. We couldn't choose, so we prayed for wisdom, we prayed to our all knowing, Almighty God! We prayed and prayed and finally came to the decision to go ahead with the biopsy, but we believed that God would protect the baby and let the doctors get their tests done to find out what was affecting Glori. After telling the specialists our decision, they told Glori that they would do the procedure early the next day so Glori was not to eat anything after 11:00 pm.

The next day came and it was 7:00 am. They asked us if we were ready and we said, "Yes." A short time later, they told us to wait another hour. Eight o'clock came, and then nine, ten, eleven, twelve and nothing happened. Several times, someone would come in and tell us that the doctors were getting everything ready and they would call us at the appropriate time. Keep in mind that my wife had not eaten anything and there was a baby inside her that was hungry also! Finally, around 1:00 pm, someone came in and said that the biopsy was cancelled by another specialist. The specialist also said that it was ok for Glori to eat and they would continue with the treatments plus also use some new medicine.

My son Frankie was about seven years old and he would crawl into the hospital bed with his mommy and would look at me with his big beautiful eyes, but I would see fear in them. At night, he and I would return home to an empty house. Our home was so lonely and empty without Glori! Needless to say, we all did a lot of praying, and God, in all his precious mercy gave us hope and showed us that he was with us. One night as my son Frankie and I were going home, the Lord put a scripture in my heart. As I was driving, the words seemed to penetrate my heart and give me the strength that I so much needed. I felt the words go deeply into my soul - **Romans 8:28, 31, 35, 37-39** (NIV):

> **28:** *And we know that in all things God works for the good of those who love him, who have been called according to his purpose.*
> **31:** *What, then, shall we say in respond to this? If God is for us, who can be against us?*
> **35:** *Who shall separate us from the love of Christ? Shall trouble or hardship or persecution or famine or nakedness or danger or sword?*

37-39: *No, in all these things we are more than conquerors through him who loved us. For I am convinced that neither death nor life, neither angels nor demons, neither the present nor the future, nor any powers, neither height nor depth, nor anything else in all creation, will be able to separate us from the love of God that is in Christ Jesus our Lord.*

I couldn't wait to get home and call my wife to share it with her (we didn't have cell phones back then). When I finally got home, I called Glori to tell her that the Lord had given me a scripture but she was already all excited because she was also so anxious to tell me that the Lord had given her a word also! When I told her the scripture that the Lord had put in my heart, she cried with joy. Amazingly, she said that it was the same scripture that the Lord had given to her! Praise the Lord!

Glori finally got out of the hospital about six weeks later. Throughout this time until the birth of the baby, the doctors or nurses were taking sonograms to make sure the baby was alright. During one of these times, God showed us another sign that everything was going to be ok. One day, as the nurse was doing the sonogram, she got a glimpse of the baby's face and the nurse shouted, "Look, the baby is smiling!" It was so encouraging! It was like the little unborn baby was saying, "I'm hanging on in here, all is well, you guys hang on out there also, God is in control!"

It seemed that all was going to be fine; the pregnancy was going well and my school work in college was going great. By mid December, I had had taken my finals and all my college work was finished. I became the first in my family to ever have received a college education. I graduated in the top twenty percent of all the students in the Computer Sciences and in the top fifteen percent of the Business College and was asked to join two honor societies. I was so ready to receive a baby girl for my graduation present!

Then, my son got sick. He got sicker and sicker and I took him to the doctor. They admitted him to the hospital because of possible rheumatic fever. My wife was getting closer to her delivery date, but I had to leave her at home so I could stay with my son at the hospital day and night since he was just a little boy. The doctors strictly told us not to let my wife come near my son for any reason since she was pregnant and was still delicate from all that she had gone through.

One day, our neighbors came to the hospital to see how Frankie was doing. As we were visiting, I noticed someone came and stood at the doorway, it was my wife! She told me she was having contractions. I asked our neighbors if they could stay with my son while I took Glori to the hospital in Amarillo and they said that they were more than happy to help out. The contractions turned out to be false labor pains so I took my wife home and went back to the hospital with my son.

I finally got to take my son home on Christmas Eve. We had a very good Christmas with a lot to be thankful for. My son was well and was back home! Late the next day, Glori began having labor pains again and I took her to the hospital, but this time I left my son with my mother-in-law who was visiting us for the holidays. At the hospital, Glori got sick and developed a very high fever - again they told us that it might affect the baby. Finally, they took Glori to the delivery room and it turned out to be a difficult delivery. She went through so much. I was there with her, praying and holding her hand. Then, finally, finally, the cry of a baby! They took her and put her in a little incubator and Glori told me, "Go see if we really had a little girl." Indeed it was, a beautiful little baby girl!

But then, the doctors told us that they had to take her into the Intensive Care Unit for infants because she wasn't breathing right and had developed strep throat. They also had to take samples from her little spinal cord with a needle. Furthermore, they had to put her under violet lights because she turned yellow (jaundice). She looked so tiny and helpless in that little incubator with her eyes wrapped with gauze and bandages so the lights wouldn't affect them.

Needless to say, again, we did a lot of praying and crying during these times. Glori was released from the hospital but we went home without our baby girl. They told us that she would have to stay for at least six more weeks.

Lord, I Hurt So Much!

Every day we would visit our little baby girl to feed her, hold her, talk to her and pray for her. It was so hard every time we had to leave the hospital without our daughter. Throughout this time, we had such beautiful pastors from our church that would come to the hospital to see us and pray for us; Reverend Billy and Bettye NIckell. One day, as we were holding our little girl, our pastors were there and we were praying and crying together. Suddenly sister Nickell turned and began speaking to our little girl and in her sweet voice said something like, "You are so precious, such a precious little girl and you are so blessed and you are going to go home with your mom and dad and you will meet your big brother at home... ...you are so precious, yes you are, yes you are."

At this point, we were all crying and then noticed that our baby girl was so focused, looking at sister Nickell as she was speaking. Our little girl had such an attentive look as if she was absorbing everything our pastor's wife was saying. We were so touched by this that we started laughing and crying at the same time! What a precious sight!

The next day, a nurse with whom we had found favor with, told us that she was going to see what she could do about letting us take our baby home since she said she noticed that we were taking very good care of our baby. She asked us how we felt about giving our baby shots (injections) because she needed injections every four hours, day and night for two more weeks. We said we could do it and after a while, the nurse came back and told us we could take our little girl home - our little bundle of joy, our little miracle, or rather our BIG MIRACLE!

Throughout tribulation, sickness, peril, throughout all odds, she hung on!

We named her Jasmine Marie Cordova. Jasmine is such a beautiful joyous girl that loves to laugh and have fun. She loves music very much; and I mention this because the doctors said that all the treatments that she went through could affect her hearing. We praise God because it didn't affect it at all. She listens to music and can learn a song very fast! Above all, she loves her

Heavenly Father - our precious Father that protected her through so many tribulations!

We went through a lot that year, but God gave us four big miracles:

1. High grades in college and high honors throughout great stress

2. My wife Glori being healed in spite of such great odds. After losing so much weight when she was sick, she gained her weight back and looked so great, she still does!

3. My son Frankie's healing, with no side effects from the rheumatic fever since the doctors had said that it could affect his heart. He became a track star and a cross country runner in high school and did three years of active duty in the United States Air Force right out of High School to serve our country. He is now in the Air Force Reserves and is a pre-med student at the University of Texas At Dallas.

4. And I got my graduating present, a beautiful baby girl, so full of life and laughter with a big heart in helping others and loves God so much! She has helped us out in prison ministry since she was five or six years old. She also has a servant's heart and helps us minister to the homeless in the inner city of Amarillo. Jasmine is also part of the praise team in the church that we pastor; using her beautiful voice to praise God!

I almost lost my entire family that year, but God Almighty had other plans. We are more than conquerors. We are more than conquerors through him who loved us - through the love of God that sent his only son for us and to the Lord Jesus for loving us so much and giving us his all by dying for us.

We are more than conquerors for our Lord wiped away our tears and showed us that he wasn't through with us yet, the same as he isn't through with you yet, brother or sister that reads this book. Read again carefully the verses that the Lord put in our hearts when my wife Glori was in the hospital: **Romans 8:28, 31, 35, 37-39** (NIV):

> **28:** *And we know that in all things God works for the good of those who love him, who have been called according to his purpose.*
> **31:** *What, then, shall we say in respond to this? If God is for us, who can be against us?*
> **35:** *Who shall separate us from the love of Christ? Shall trouble or hardship or persecution or famine or nakedness or danger or sword?*
> **37-39:** *No, in all these things we are more than conquerors through him who loved us. For I am convinced that neither death nor life, neither angels nor demons, neither the present nor the future, nor any powers, neither height nor depth, nor anything else in all creation, will be able to separate us from the love of God that is in Christ Jesus our Lord.*

Prayer: *Precious Lord, you comfort me in perilous times, you give me strength in times of weakness. I thank you for the stories in this chapter for I can see that you made us to be more than conquerors - to conquer fear and doubt and to conquer anything that tries to separate us from you. I will conquer trouble and hardship with your precious help. I learned that the author of this book almost lost his whole family in one year, but you had better plans for this family and I know that you have plans for me also, good plans! Even though I may not understand some things as I am going through them, but I trust that you will work them for the good. Thank you my Lord Jesus, in your powerful name, Amen.*

Unit III - Chapter 10

Time To Let Go

*To every thing there is a season,
and a time to every purpose under the heaven:
A time to weep, and a time to laugh;
a time to mourn, and a time to dance.
Ecclesiastes 3:1, 4 (KJV)*

When is it time to let go of the past? When is it time to let go of the hurt?

Let us suppose that you are a marathon runner in the Olympics. You have trained your body very hard to be able to withstand the demands to push it to finish the distance of about 26 miles (about 42 kilometers). You have followed a strict diet and have planned out your strategy on how you are going to win this race. Then, the day of the great Olympian race is here and you are ready for it. You know that you are in the best shape you've ever been and you feel excellent that day. Many have shown up for the race and the crowd is pumped. You're ready at the starting line and the gun goes off to start the race. You start out great and have developed a very good stride plus your breathing is perfect. You start to pull away from the rest of the runners. As time progresses, you notice that you are in first place and you're doing very well on time with just a few more miles to go. The people

Lord, I Hurt So Much!

are cheering as you pass by. They call out your name. There is a smile on your face as you realize that the person in second place is at least two miles behind you and the person in third place is about a mile or two behind him. You can feel the thrill of victory as you have three or four more miles to go. That gold medal is just around the corner. But all of a sudden, from the cheering crowd, a man runs out and grabs you and pushes you into the crowd! You can't believe what just happened. Why did he do that? He breaks your stride and your concentration. Where are the police? Suddenly, someone from the crowd tackles him and then picks you up to help you get back in the race. You try to run and concentrate on the race as before, but the damage is done. The shock of what just happened is affecting the way you think. As the finish line is approaching, the person that was in second place passes you and not too long after that, the person that was in third place passes you as well. The race ends and you come in third. There is a deep disappointment in the crowd and around the world as television stations keep showing the scene where the man in the crowd jumps out and pushes you into the crowd. Your country cries out for justice and quickly points out that you would have won the race if the spectator had not interfered. The Olympic judges claim that there is no way to determine that and there is nothing that they can do. There is nothing that anybody can do. The damage is done.

What do you do? Do you side with your country and the crowd or for that matter, the whole world and demand justice? Do you become angry for what happened? As the days turn into weeks and the weeks into months and everyone that sees you says that you are a victim of injustice, do you become even angrier? Do you become bitter?

Should we see what a runner did when this really happened to him? Yes, this happened in real life! During the 2004 Olympics, the Brazilian runner Vanderlei de Lima was pushed by a spectator as Vanderlei was leading the race[1]. De Lima wound up winning the bronze medal as he was passed by Stefano Baldini from Italy, then by Mebrahtom Keflezighi from the United States.

Lord, I Hurt So Much!

What I would like to emphasize here is Vanderlei's attitude. He could have fought a bitter fight and claimed that he would have won the gold medal if it wasn't for the interference, but he humbly accepted the bronze. Another Brazilian athlete that won a gold metal (Emanuel Rego) gave de Lima his gold medal but Vanderlei de Lima gave it back to him and humbly said, "I can't accept Emanuel's medal. I'm happy with mine, it's bronze but means gold"[2]. Not only did his words touch me, but as I saw clips of the marathon, my eyes swelled up with tears as Vanderlie came into the Athens stadium at the end of the race with his hands extended like an airplane. He zigzaged back and forth as a big smile shined from his face. He lifted his hands up in triumph then he threw kisses with both hands to the crowd in the stadium that was cheering for him. Vanderlie de Lima also received the Pierre de Coubertin medal for his sportsmanship[3]; a very high honor.

His attitude displayed that even though he was attacked and disrupted on his road to his goal, nothing was going to take away the victory in the end. Even though he didn't finish in first place as he pictured he would but he did finish the race; he got back in and ran the race. Even though he didn't receive the prize that he was planning on winning which was a gold medal, in his mind, his prize was gold. He also received another award that showed his character. But I believe that the prize that pushed him over the top was his attitude. No bitterness, no regrets and the whole world cheered him on. Many articles have been written about him and many sermons have been preached about his attitude.

Another person that has touched my life with his attitude is Horatio Spafford. As several tragedies filled his life, he took comfort in the Lord and wrote a beautiful poem that was later turned into a beloved hymn. The hymn itself has a gentle tune that calms the heart and brings peace to the soul. The words speak of taking refuge in the Lord Jesus Christ through the many trials. But knowing the background of how it came about brings strength and hope as this treasure flowed from Horatio Spafford's heart.

Spafford was a wealthy lawyer that lived in Chicago with his wife, four daughters and a son in the 1870's. Through his law practice and his investments in real estate, he became very prosperous. Then tragedy struck when his son died at the very young age of four. Not long after that, the great Chicago fire consumed all his properties. He later decided to take a trip to Europe with his wife and daughters on a ship. Business plans delayed him so he sent his family on ahead as he planned to join them later. As the ship sailed the Atlantic Ocean, the ship that his family was traveling on collided with another ship and sank very quickly. His wife survived but his four daughters drowned in the cold ocean. His wife sent Spafford a telegram with just two words, "Saved alone". As Spafford crossed the ocean to meet with his wife in England, he wrote the words to the cherished hymn "It Is Well With My Soul"[4].

It Is Well With My Soul

When peace like a river, attendeth my way,
When sorrows like sea billows roll;
Whatever my lot, Thou hast taught me to say,
It is well, it is well, with my soul.

Refrain:
It is well, with my soul,
It is well, with my soul,
It is well, it is well, with my soul.

Though Satan should buffet, though trials should come,
Let this blest assurance control,
That Christ has regarded my helpless estate,
And hath shed His own blood for my soul.

My sin, oh, the bliss of this glorious thought!
My sin, not in part but the whole,
Is nailed to the cross, and I bear it no more,
Praise the Lord, praise the Lord, O my soul!

For me, be it Christ, be it Christ hence to live:
If Jordan above me shall roll,
No pang shall be mine, for in death as in life,
Thou wilt whisper Thy peace to my soul.

But Lord, 'tis for Thee, for Thy coming we wait,
The sky, not the grave, is our goal;
Oh, trump of the angel! Oh, voice of the Lord!
Blessed hope, blessed rest of my soul.

And Lord, haste the day when my faith shall be sight,
The clouds be rolled back as a scroll;
The trump shall resound, and the Lord shall descend,
Even so, it is well with my soul.

Horatio Spafford[5]

There comes a time to let go of the pain and suffering that has come into our lives. There is a season when we must decide not to carry that load anymore; just drop it and not carry it ever again! It's not so much that it won't ever come back to our memory again, but that we should let go of the pain that it reminds us of.

Whether to let go of the pain in a victory dance and not focus on the tragedy like Vanderlei de Lima or by letting out the pain in a gentle song like Horatio Spafford, it's time to let go.

Chapter three of the Book of Ecclesiastes gives us a list of events that we go through in life and it tells us that there is a beginning and an ending in all these circumstances. Although this list is by no means comprehensive, it does indicate that there is a time to everything; and thus, we can also say, "There is a time to let go".

Ecclesiastes 3:1-8 (KJV) - *To every thing there is a season, and a time to every purpose under the heaven:*
A time to be born, and a time to die; a time to plant, and a time to pluck up that which is planted;

A time to kill, and a time to heal; a time to break down, and a time to build up;
A time to weep, and a time to laugh; a time to mourn, and a time to dance;
A time to cast away stones, and a time to gather stones together; a time to embrace, and a time to refrain from embracing;
A time to get, and a time to lose; a time to keep, and a time to cast away;
A time to rend, and a time to sew; a time to keep silence, and a time to speak;
A time to love, and a time to hate; a time of war, and a time of peace.

I would like to emphasize **verse 4**: *A time to weep, and a time to laugh; a time to mourn, and a time to dance.* Throughout all your hurt, you have already wept, now it's time to laugh. In all your afflictions, you have mourned, now it's time to dance! I'm not talking about going out to a ball to dance and drink punch, but a dance of joy and gratification, giving praise to God - giving the Lord honor and appreciation, celebrating that the weeping and sadness are now in the past.

Prayer: *Beloved God in heaven, I praise and glorify your name. I now drop each and every burden at your feet and I won't pick them up anymore; it's time to let go of all the pain and sorrow. Thank you for the new direction that you now point me to. I will follow your perfect plan that you have for me. It's time to let go of all my hurt. I turn over my crushed heart to you. I have wept, I have had sadness and sorrow, but now I will have nothing but praise on my lips; praises for you dear Lord, for you have taken away my afflictions. I love you so much. Thank you that you are with me. I pray in the name of your beloved son Jesus Christ. Amen.*

Unit III - Chapter 11

The God Of Love And Peace Will Be With You

*Finally, brethren, farewell.
Be perfect, be of good comfort,
be of one mind, live in peace;
and the God of love and peace shall be with you.
2 Corinthians 13:11 (KJV)*

As the end of this book approaches, I hope and pray that you have come to a place where your hurt is mending or has mended. The conclusion to a hurting situation is to seek God. In my life where I have gone through many painful situations, the answer has been prayer or prayer together with fasting.

As stated before, sometimes the process is very slow. There will be times when praying is so difficult and nothing can really be expressed, but keep pressing on. We have a promise that the Holy Spirit will intercede for us.

Romans 8:26 (NIV) - *In the same way, the Spirit helps us in our weakness. We do not know what we ought to pray for, but the Spirit himself intercedes for us through workless groans.*

The Holy Spirit intercedes for us. He knows our pain. He knows our needs. He will give us the strength. This is the same Spirit that raised Jesus from the dead (**Romans 8:11**), he is the same that will help you out. He is the same that will raise you from your affliction.

God will not get tired of helping you and me. Let's read what Isaiah the prophet wrote about the everlasting God in **Isaiah 40:28-31** (NIV).

Do you not know? Have you not heard? The Lord is the everlasting God, the Creator of the ends of the earth. He will not grow tired or weary, and his understanding no one can fathom. He gives strength to the weary and increases the power of the weak. Even youths grow tired and weary, and young men stumble and fall; but those who hope in the Lord will renew their strength. They will soar on wings like eagles; they will run and not grow weary, they will walk and not be faint.

As you are on the road to recovery from a broken heart, I would give you some advice - "remember!" Remember what situations hurt you. Remember the words that hurt you; the mean things that someone said or the names that were called out. Remember the awful jokes that were played that were very degrading. Let us remember all this, because in doing so, we remember how much they hurt us, so we don't hurt others. Also remember that they can also hurt others and you can be there to help the ones that are afflicted.

Our Lord Jesus Christ teaches us this principal in **Matthew 7:12** (NIV), which we have learned as "The Golden Rule":

So in everything, do to others what you would have them do to you, for this sums up the Law and the Prophets.

I heard a story somewhere about James Cash Penney, the founder of the J. C. Penney stores where he believed in the Golden Rule. He called his employees "associates" making them feel equal to him instead of beneath him. He also treated his customers as he wanted to be treated; with respect. The people responded well to this kind of attitude and he made quite a fortune - because of respect. We can see that even today it is still paying off because even though he is not living anymore, his stores are still around in so many places.

When we put ourselves in another person's shoes, we get a greater perspective on how to be a better person; we can see how people like to be treated. We will never understand each and every situation nor will we ever understand every person, but we can work at it one person at a time.

Now that we have prayed and fasted and gone through this book and have been strengthen by the Lord, we can help others. We can now be more effective in helping others that have gone through the same situations that we have.

We should lend a hand when we can and receive it when one is offered, together with the mighty hand of God we can heal the people that have said, "Lord I hurt so much!"

In our final prayer, we pray together with the apostle Paul in **Ephesians 3:16-21** (NIV):

I pray that out of his glorious riches he may strengthen you with power through his Spirit in your inner being, so that Christ may dwell in your hearts through faith. And I pray that you, being rooted and established in love, may have power, together with all the Lord's holy people, to grasp how wide and long and high and deep is the love of Christ, and to know this love that surpasses knowledge—that you may be filled to the measure of all the fullness of God. Now to him who is able to do immeasurably more than all we ask or imagine, according to his power that is at work within us, to him be glory in the church and in Christ Jesus throughout all generations, for ever and ever! Amen.

Credits

KJV	King James Version © Copyright 1983 by Holman Bible Publishers. All rights reserved.
NIV	New International Version Scripture taken from the HOLY BIBLE, NEW INTERNATIONAL VERSION ®, Copyright © 1973, 1978, 1984 by International Bible Society

Unit I
Chapter 1
1 Stevenson, Mary. "Footprints in the Sand". Footprints in the Sand. http://www.footprints-inthe-sand.com/index.php?page=Poem/Poem.php. (16 Nov 2010).

Unit II
Unit II Page
1 Wikipedia The Free Encyclopedia. "Serenity Prayer". Serenity Prayer - Wikipedia, the free encyclopedia. http://en.wikipedia.org/wiki/Serenity_Prayer (23 Feb 2011).

Jasmine's Picture (middle of book)
2 Olan Mills Studio. Jasmine Cordova. Olan Mills Studio, Amarillo Used by permission.

Chapter 6
2 "To Every Man An Answer". *To Every Man An Answer.* Christian Satellite Network Radio. KAWZ, Sioux Falls. 6 June 2011. Radio.

Unit III
Chapter 8
1 Merriam-Webster. "divisive". <u>An Encylopaedia Britannica Company Merriam-Wester</u>. http://www.merriam-webster.com/dictionary/divisive (18 Sep 2011).
2 <u>Rocky III</u>. Dir. Sylvester Stallone. Writ. Sylvester Stallone. Perf. Sylvester Stallone, Talia Shire, Burt Young, Carl Weathers, Mr. T. Chartoff-Winkler Productions, United Artists, 1982.

Chapter 10
1 Wikipedia The Free Encyclopedia. "Vanderlei de Lima". <u>Vanderlei de Lima From Wikipedia, the free encyclopedia</u>. http://en.wikipedia.org/wiki/Vanderlei_de_Lima (11 Aug 2011).

2 et al

3 et al

4 Wikipedia The Free Encyclopedia. "It Is Well With My Soul". <u>It Is Well With My Soul From Wikipedia, the free encyclopedia</u>. http://en.wikipedia.org/wiki/It_Is_Well_with_My_Soul (11 Aug 2011).

5 et al

Back cover picture by Shane Moore Photography
www.shanemoorephotography.smugmug.com

www.ingramcontent.com/pod-product-compliance
Ingram Content Group UK Ltd.
Pitfield, Milton Keynes, MK11 3LW, UK
UKHW041949230426
12048UKWH00008B/228